I0558109

Study

Hacks

How to Study and Retain Everything Without Spending Hours Studying

(Ultimate Strategy to Become a Topper Forever)

Charles Stallings

Published By **Ryan Princeton**

Charles Stallings

Study Hacks: How to Study and Retain Everything Without Spending Hours Studying (Ultimate Strategy to Become a Topper Forever)

ISBN 978-1-998927-11-1

No part of this guidebook shall be reproduced in any form without permission in writing from the publisher except in the case of brief quotations embodied in critical articles or reviews.

Legal & Disclaimer

Table Of Contents

Chapter 1: How to "Read" Two to Four Times Faster Instantly Without Speed Reading

It boggles my mind no pace studying e-book ever talks approximately this. And but comprehension is a lot higher the usage of this method. The reality is, studying is one of the most inefficient strategies to eat and keep statistics however with this approach, I name tempo-listening, you won't even want to take the time to "test" and endure in mind.

I'm speakme about being attentive to audio books into 4 times the actual velocity. Just do this, down load a software called VLC participant, (Google it) after which open an audio ebook, or an audio lecture, or a film, after that right click on on in the middle of the show, and pick "playback", after which select" faster" and pay attention to the 1.5x pace-upped audio. You will locate some issue thrilling, the audio stays very lots understandable even at 50% faster pace. In fact, it makes the stupid ebook, or lecture, or movie even more exciting.

As a give up result, nowadays, I never be aware of any audio with out at least rushing it as a lot as at the least one.5x from the unique pace. I even watch films in 1.5x speed. Yes, I am a big nerd so I do no longer desire to waste my time on "trivial" entertainments. I want to transport decrease returned to my lab as quickly a likely and art work on new techniques to come to be a genius.

I will communicate about the charge-listening approach in detail inside the nextbankruptcy. I will speak about the way to convert your notes into audio and speed it up in advance than you load it into your iPods. I will talk approximately how you could accelerate any e-book you want via converting them into audio books. In fact, I turn every piece of facts into audio books so I can listen to them even as I am the use of, cooking, (sure women, I prepare dinner) and taking walks. As a give up stop result, I now have time for entertainment sports like sky diving, writing, flirting with the opportunity sex, getting under the influence of alcohol and blitzing via the open highways on my extremely good motorbike. A hundred miles in step with hour.

OK, earlier than we get into pace-listening and the manner it works we want to put down some floor rules.

Before we pass into the techniques of rapid-studying, velocity-listening, Feynman strategies and loads of greater...you want to understand a few key foundation thoughts first.

First, the purpose of this ebook is to make fast-studying easy and easy. We can gather this goal with the useful aid of using easy strategies/techniques that does not require hundreds of time and , most importantly, strategies that does not require plenty information to grasp.

A suitable example can be the tempo-listening technique mentioned within the preceding financial disaster. Why spend time and effort mastering pace studying while you may pay interest faster with higher comprehension? There's no cause to.

As you are probable beaten thru the stacks of required readings already, there may be no thing in learning complicated, time eating and plenty less powerful study strategies. This ebook includes the maximum inexperienced and effective have a look at techniques that I apprehend of.

OK, shall we've got were given a have a look at a few big photo mind, earlier than we get into the techniques itself, I want you to pay interest and actively show yourself on the onesmind under:

•I already knew this

•I disagree/I do now not consider this may paintings

The abovethoughts are the maximum important barriers to reading a few factor. Chances are, a number of the mind in this ebook will sound familiar. You ought to probably have even discovered or look at about it someplace. However, via telling yourself that you already knew this, you may leave out out on a few important statistics. There is probably a few small but crucial differences in my strategies that you can glance through.

Also, now not believing a particular technique will paintings as promised will most effective restrict your learning capability. The fine manner to find out if a method works is to test it out your self. Some of the strategies would possibly sound ridiculous but so are maximum new thoughts or paradigm.

Next, I focus masses on techniques that enhance information in vicinity of rote memorization. There's a variety of motives for this but essentially it's miles because of the fact rote memorization is painful, time-losing, and vain most of the time. Once you understand a subject deeply, you may with out problem maintain in thoughts it for a very long term.

Of route, I will cover some memorization strategies which are easy to do however very effective. Complicated reminiscence techniques much like the memory-palace is over-kill for our reason.

And in the end, please do not over complicate the techniques through adding greater steps on top of it. Human beings will be inclined to over optimize. If it ain't broken do not repair it. And if you want to "repair" it then draw close the fundamentals first.

Let me offer you with an example, let's imagine you've got got a Lexus and it runs remarkable. Optimizing it with the aid of converting a larger tires, better gas injection tool and possibly an ostrich leather-based-based dashboard will now not make it masses greater snug, or quicker by using the usage of the usage of a big margin.

But if you have a Tata Nano, that is a small and reasonably-priced automobile, then upgrading it to a Lexus will make a large difference in consolation, tempo, strength, acceleration, protection and so forth.

The techniques on this ebook is "Lexus" so do no longer waste a while searching for to optimize it in advance than you may maximize it.

The blessings of consuming information at a tempo faster than "ordinary studying tempo" have to be apparent. Cutting your studying time with the beneficial aid of as a minimum half is one of the essential advantages. Who wants to spend extra time reading dry books? I as an alternative spend my time on devouring exciting books.

But there may be one issue benefit to rush-listening that many do not talk approximately, the benefit of getting a dry state of affairs/subject matter will become a excellent deal lots much less dry. Interesting, even. The subject turns into colorful and interesting due to the truth you are eating records at a quicker pace. It's like the usage of a Ferrari a hundred miles consistent with hour, on an open motorway. You revel in the adrenaline rush and you are smiling ear to eat in satisfaction. That's why I velocity pay interest like a demon.

Clinical trials have even shown that children and adults with ADD/ADHD display more comprehension, hobby, and retention of records whilst exposed to high pace audio book. OK, permit's circulate on.

First of all, as you realize, I do now not tempo look at if I can tempo-pay attention. I can speed-pay interest 600 word regular with minute with out loss of comprehension but training to have a observe 600 phrases in line with minute isn't always viable. That's because 400 phrase in line with minute is the most reading pace that superior pace reader can manipulate.

Why is that? It's certainly the mind's project. You can't take a look at greater than 400

WPM because of the fact your mind can't technique phrases faster than that. It's taxing to have a look at speedy too. Where-else you may be privy to 800 WPM without lack of comprehension. This is because of the fact our mind Is built to pay attention, now not study. We did not begin reading till approximately 600 years in the beyond. And even then, best the richest men and kings observe. Normal human beings don't examine till perhaps three hundred years within the past.

Chapter 2: How to Speed-Listen

So how do you pace-pay attention as an alternative? First of all, search for the audio versions of your textbook. They is probably available in audio or they may not. If they are in audio model then you definately actually absolutely want to hurry up the audio the use of a application known as Audio Speed Changer Pro. You can down load it at http://www.Superutils.Com/merchandise/audio-pace-changer-seasoned/.

Audio Speed Changer Pro (Henceforth known as ASCP) is the notable software application out there to rush up your audio. There are severa motives for this. One, it is clean to apply, a few clicks and changes and you are done. Second, ASCP solves the "chipmunk" voice hassle common in particular audio pace-up packages. Download a unfastened trial of ASCP and spend a couple of minutes reading the "ReadMe" report and you will be up and walking.

If you want to pay attention to your audio e book on a pc you then truly must get a unfastened software application program called VLC participant. It accelerates your audio with out the "chipmunk" sound effect too. Here's the manner to do it:

1. Open your audio document with VLC Player.

2. Right click on on in the center of the player.

3. Then pick out out "Playback" and click on "Faster". This will accelerate your audio thru 1.5x tempo. You can do the equal with movies.

4. Click "Faster" over again to rush it up even extra.

What if there can be no audio e-book to be had for the e-book you want to hurry-pay attention to? Then you have to search for the PDF, or text, or html version of the ebook.

Most of the ebook in recent times have a PDF model. Download the PDF model and open it the usage of a software called TextAloud. You can down load it at:

http://www.Nextup.Com/TextAloud/.

Again, there may be no free software program application software that does this, sorry for that. If you make a decision to buy TextAloud then you definately without a doubt definately must moreover purchase the AT&T natural voices due to the truth the default voice in TextAloud is pretty bad. Trust me, the natural voices makes a variety of distinction to your comprehension of the audio ebook.

Note: AT&T herbal voices is a shape of voice that reads the ebook to you out loud. I choose the voice of Mike from AT&T natural voices.

OK, as soon as you have downloaded TextAloud you need to open your PDF book with it.

You can then accelerate the readings through manner of manner of the use of a slider on the pinnacle right corner referred to as

"Speed". Adjust the charge till you're snug with it.

And now, if you need to hurry-pay interest on your laptop you can sincerely press "Play". But if you need to speed-pay interest in your Ipod then you need to click on on "speak to report".

This will preserve an mp3 or .Wmv audio report into your laptop. (You can pick the file layout, depending for your music player)

For Existing Audio Book

So allow's recap. If there may be an audio model of your e-book, you can velocity it up the usage of ASCP, and then concentrate to it on an ipod.

Or, if you opt to pay interest for your audio ebook on a pc, then you can use the VLC player to hurry it up.

For Book Without Audio Book Available

If there may be no audio book to be had to your textbook, but you had access to the PDF,

HTML, and text layout of your e-book, then you may use TextAloud to speed-deliver attention to both the ipod and your laptop.

And ultimately, what if there may be no audio, video, text, HTML or maybe PDF format available for the e-book you need to rush-pay attention to?

If it in reality is the case then you don't have any preference but to install writing notes. I will cowl take a look at writing on this e-book later. For now, virtually understand that observe writing can be very powerful in comprehension and cutting once more time in studying. Anyway, write your notes in a text file and use TextAloud to transform it into audio. Remember to hurry it up earlier than you convert it to audio documents.

OK, permit's go through the whole thing step by step.

If you've got the audio model e-book:

1. Use Audio Speed Changer Pro to hurry up the audio - down load it at:

http://www.Superutils.Com/merchandise/au dio-pace-changer-seasoned/

2. Save the audio file

three. Download the audio file into your portable player of desire

four. Enjoy taking note of 1.5x tempo or more, with out learning the way to rush look at and with more comprehension.

If you have got the audio version book and want to pay attention for your audio in your computer:

1. Download VLC participant at:

 http://www.Videolan.Org/vlc/index.Html

2. open your audio e-book

three. Right click on on on in the middle, and hover your mouse to "Playback", after which click on on on on "Faster".

There's additionally a "quicker (splendid)" option, which top notch quickens your audio through the use of using 0.1 in step with click on on, while "Faster" boost up your audio via zero.Five. You also can maintain clicking "Faster" to rush up your audio even more.

4. enjoy.

If you simplest have the PDF, textual content, or HTMl model of your e-book then:

1. down load TextAloud from:

http://www.Nextup.Com/TextAloud/

2. Also purchase the AT&T voice of Mike. (Recommended)

three. Use TextAloud to open the PDF/text/html file

four. Press play, then go to the "speed" slider in your pinnacle proper and accelerate the audio.

5. Keep on finding out the velocity until it's miles fast but comprehensible.

6. in case you're taking note of your laptop then you definitely clearly truely do no longer want to do something else.

But if you're planning to be aware of the audio on your portable music player then follow the 2 steps below.

•Click "Speak to report", it is simply below the "Speed" slider and maintain your file.

•Upload the mp3 or wmv audio record into your portable track player.

And, in case you do now not have all the above, then you definately definately ought to write notes and upload the notes into TextAloud.

The velocity-listening method may be used to have a look at almost a few issue which include mathematics. Of direction, you can not concentrate to math proofs on audio however you could in truth concentrate to the theories.

Bonus: Listening is a outstanding way to maintain time and rentain more of what you have got found out. However, a higher manner is to each concentrate and have a look at. According to investigate, the greater senses you comprise whilst eating facts, the greater facts you may keep. For example, you could preserve in mind extra via way of looking a multimedia slides with video, phrases and sound, in choice to honestly reading.

And if you include all your senses like contact, scent, imaginative and prescient, and taking note of then you definitely truely sincerely should've maximized your hazard of remembering the cloth. This is why you recall greater even as you "do stuff", as opposed to simply analyzing approximately them. Practical courses like dissecting a frog is lots extra memorable, do not you agree?

With that said, use TextAloud to open a report and examine it on the equal time you pay interest. The black cursor will bounce from phrase to word, so that you can tempo-pay attention to it at the equal time.

Chapter 3: The Logical Note-Taking

There is a pc sickness that all and sundry who works with laptop structures is aware of about. It's a completely severe disease and it interferes simply with the paintings. The hassle with computer systems is which you 'play' with them!

- Richard Feynman

Taking proper notes is essential for know-how the problem depend, reviewing, and business enterprise of information for clean retrieval. Your notes also may be converted into audio for listening on down-times. (Down instances are searching for advice from instances in that you're unable to do some element else, but need to be there even though, things like jogging, commercial breaks or maybe cooking.)

But probably the most essential purpose to have a based have a look at is due to the fact you want to have a goal. What do I suggest thru that? Let me offer an motive for.

Without a smooth aim on what shape of data to extract from a category, you'll pay interest passively. With passive listening, you may no longer take in tons, if any, records.

Passive listening isn't always the absence of awareness or hobby. It is simply listening without information how and in which, on your mind, to vicinity the go along with the go with the flow of new facts. It's like watching a film VS reading the way to restore a computer.

When you watch a film, you're truely sitting on a couch, interesting and no longer doing an awful lot, if any, questioning in any respect. That's passive. But if you're analyzing how to restore a damaged computer then you definately definately have a smooth intention on what information you could need, the troubleshooting you have carried out, trial and errors, symptoms and signs to pay interest on, and so forth.

However, maximum of the notes I've visible haven't any shape, are messy, and hard to read. Most importantly, most students does no longer draw near the huge idea and the factors of the topic.

Big Ideas & Elements

But what do I mean via massive thoughts and elements of the difficulty? The big idea is surely the notion or the precis of the subject to be had. For instance, the big concept for the theory of evolution is "survival of the fittest."

The factors is how the large concept is established to be proper. In the idea of the evolution, Charles Darwin is going via a chain of logical steps to reach at the belief that "survival of the fittest" is how evolution occurs. Those steps are the factors.

The massive concept and the factors are crucial due to the fact the ones are all of the matters that an examination will check you on. You're given a query and also you need to list down all of the factors that ends in the large concept/stop.

Plus, that is the extremely good manner to write down down notes even in case you're not studying for an exam. For what is the motive of studying if not to get a quit give up end result (big ideas) and the "how-tos" (elements)?

In extraordinary phrases, "logical be aware taking" is logical because of the truth you only jot down the critical statistics, and located it at the right section. This way you store time and effort.

Also, taking notes sell energetic listening in preference to passive listening. With lively listening you are actively listening for wallet-of-content material material that you may categorize. This method you pay greater hobby in elegance and absorb extra information as a give up result.

Where else with passive listening you are not going to hold in thoughts a whole lot and there may be no motive in your listening. Class is boring and it's far hard to inspire yourself to wait instructions.

OK, right here's what you need to do as a way to take right notes. First, you need to go to each elegance. It does not rely if you've partied the complete night time and drank a barrel of alcohol. Nothing beats attending class for pinnacle notes material.

Why? Because professors have a easy spot for tidy attendance. They will regularly talk approximately the big mind, elements, definitions and the huge questions in a subject. This saves you a whole lot of time combing via thick textbooks. Trust me, it's a pain going via textbooks trying to find all of the important facts. And as I've stated before, analyzing is painfully slow and tedious as compared to listening.

Ok, permit's go with the flow immediately to the second one schooling. You have to make use of every computer, and the pen and paper to take notes. Only use your computer to kind notes for non-technical topics like philosophy, psychology, creative writing, and so on. In extremely good phrases, publications that doesn't deal with mathematical equations. This is because laptops commonly might not have mathematical symbols on its keyboard.

But why laptop? It's surely due to the fact you kind faster on a laptop and your writing can be plenty greater readable. Also, loose software software program like TreeDBNotes organizes your notes in a logical tree-like format. With TreeDBNotes, you could locate facts the use of the quest feature and there can be numerous formating preference to highlight critical elements.

As I stated in advance than you have to use pen and paper for technical scenario like maths, engineering and physics. It's more tough to installation your paper notes however a smooth method is to prepare a committed folder for every elegance that you attend. Don't need to get too fancy, a clean and plain folder is sufficient.

Now, lets get began on a manner to take proper notes.

First of all, reading in favored is all approximately identifying the massive thoughts, if the author of the ebook does now not provide it, after which explaining, and contrasting the big idea with different, opposing massive mind. And in the end reevaluate it, in slight of recent proof.

For example, the concept of evolution (huge idea) may be contrasted in opposition to the idea of nurturing. The concept of evolution can be defined due to the fact the exchange in the inherited trends of organic populations over successive generations.

And in the end, in slight of new evidence from Quantum physics the idea of evolution desires to be reevaluated. Note:These are clearly examples that I made up.

Also, you need to format your notes intently, so as for crucial factors and sections to face out. Bolding, capitalizing, skipping lines to create white place, growing font length, the use of asterisks, and bullets factors for critical elements. This make your notes easier to have a look at and consume.

And subsequently, use labels like lecture titles, dates, :EXCEPTION:, :DEF: (for definitions), and and plenty of others.

Definitions and Big Questions

OK, we have mentioned factors and the huge concept, and that they act just like the sections of your notes. Theseare the most critical sections but they're not sufficient. To have an tremendous be conscious you ought to haveunique sections, that is the questions and definitions.

Questions is the question or questions that ends in the conclusions. It's just like the hypothesis of a precept. This is how maximum scientist begins an studies proper right into a concept, and it is no twist of destiny that that is how your professor commonly thinks. Almost all of the professor that I've encountered assume in questions. So you need to extract the questions, hidden or not, from the lectures.

As for definitions, it's far sincerely the motive of jargons or definitions for unusual or new terms. This is crucial for information your textual content. Not statistics jargons or definitions is like listening to a overseas language. You don't have any idea what is taking vicinity.

So to recap, we have 4 factors that desires to be located in all of your non-technical publications notes. They are the factors, huge thoughts, definitions, and questions. These four factors are typically observed in all of my notes except for technical guides. Let's talk how this will artwork in each non-technical publications and technical path.

Non-Technical Courses Note-Taking

Open the TreeDBNote software program (exceptionally advocated loose software program software) and label the pinnacle node as your lecture's name. Then create four infant nodes underneath the top node, categorized questions, big mind, factors, and definitions.

The most essential piece of information is the large concept. Like I said, it is the summarization of the complete concept. And you need to be able to provide an purpose of it, assessment it, and re-examine it in light of new evidence in advance than you exams.

Unfortunately, it is subsequent to not possible to get the big mind from studying a book for your very personal. It might also take an excessive amount of effort and time. If you are like me, you're pressed for time as it is. The incredible way to get the big thoughts is to wait the lecture classes.

This is the high-quality and most green way. Of path, most teachers will no longer will can help you understand the massive mind up the the front, and that they've an inclination to ramble and digress. However, it is easy to pick out out the huge mind by using way of identifying positive key terms.

Lecturers or professors will regularly say the ones words beneath earlier than introducing a large idea.

•so in summary...

•meaning...

•the notion is...

•therefore, the answer for the question is...

•the eliminate is...

•proper right here's the crucial factor...

Or any of the model above. Don't worry if you can not understand the huge concept on the begin. You'll get it, through the years.

And in advance than I forget about, you should in no way write the entirety verbatim. The notes need to be uniquely yours. It does not even be counted number range if one-of-a-kind people might no longer recognize what you wrote. And, simply as a reminder, format your notes closely. If you cannot make experience of your notes from scanning it, then the formatting is not correct enough.

And you ought to additionally shop every word inner a dated folder. The form want to look like this:

Class/topic Folder >> Dates as folder call >> Class Topics as names in TreeDBNotes layout.

This is only for organizational sake.

To recap, the form of your notes ought to be Questions, Elements, Big thoughts, and Definitions. And they all should have their very very own "notes" in a tree-like hierarchy style in TreeDBNotes. If there can be sub-questions, sub-factors, sub-definitions, and sub-huge-thoughts then they all should be one degree below their respective category like this:

[class topic name]

[big ideas]

[sub-big ideas]

[questions]

[sub questions]

What do I suggest by means of "sub-big-thoughts"? It's really the secondary large ideas. For example, the big idea for this chapter (the e-book you are reading now) is the concept of getting 4 categories for word-taking. The sub-massive-ideas may be non-technical word-taking and technical be conscious taking. Thetopic are associated but precise sufficient to stand on their very own as sub-classes. With that said, permit's bypass at once to...

Technical Courses Note Taking

By technical path, I endorse courses like mathematics, calculus, technology, engineering and and so forth. Basically the guides that address equations closely. It's some distance much less difficult to put in writing notes for technical publications and more difficult on the identical time. Let me provide an explanation for.

For technical publications, you may not be using a pc but pen and paper as an opportunity due to the fact there's no keyboard optimized for typing equations and formulas. This is the tougher-issue. The nicely facts is that it is a lot less complicated. There's no shape concerned. There's only factors and exclusive causes of the involved troubles. In distinctive terms, it's far all approximately examples after examples of the formula in motion. Your procedure is to put in writing down each instance given inside the lecture.

You can forget about about approximately the huge mind, questions, or maybe definitions. The "factors" or "steps" is the most crucial factor to install writing. Again, attending each elegance is crucial because of the reality all off the crucial techniques and components are included in the elegance. There's clearly no want to have a study the text e-book.

However, that does not propose textual content books are not required at all. It's beneficial to convey your text books to the magnificence and use it to bypass reference what has been said inside the beauty. Comparing how your professor training consultation the steps and the way it is laid out inside the ebook.

So to recap:

•write down the troubles and the answers. (Elements)

•Ask all your questions sooner or later of the class if you do no longer understand. Don't leave your questions for "later".

•try and get the entirety executed within the elegance, and I advocate all homework too in amongst commands and in awesome lessons. This will prevent masses of time. (This will be similarly noted in the time management monetary disaster)

One a aspect phrase, you need to have a look at all your notes right after elegance. This is crucial because of the reality you forget about 50% to 80% of what you have determined out after 24 hours, and because of the reality you need to make your corrections and additions on the equal time as it's miles though sparkling in your mind. OK, please flip the page to the subsequent financial catastrophe.

Chapter 4: Self Management VS Time Management

Not dealing with some time and making excuses arebad conduct. Don't located them every together via claiming you "do now not have the time".

- Bo Bennett

What's self manipulate you ask? It's virtually time manage however due to the fact time control is a bit of a misnomer, I've determined to call this chapter self manage. What do I advocate? Let me provide an motive at the back of.

Time manage is a misnomer because of the fact you can not control time. How are you able to manipulate "time" at the same time as time continues on ticking irrespective of what you do? You can "manage some time" till your face is blue and it will slip thru your like sand passing through the cracks of your hands.

You can, but, control yourself. And if you do an remarkable project at it then the effects of your tests might be super. Very unique.

First of all, studies has showed that pressure reduces your learning capability through the use of a massive margin. Why? Because the blood waft on your mind is reduced substantially.

Stress have an impact on your frame in which includes a manner as to redirecting the majority of your blood to "important" locations, like your legs and coronary heart. This made enjoy in case you're on foot far from a tiger, it truly is one of the only some situations our ancestors are confused out about.

So what do you do? You lessen stress. How? Well, there are few approaches to do this, and the strategies listed under are the nice pressure-melting techniques that I apprehend of.

First, you want to get into the dependancy of meditating. It's stupid and it is difficult but it is also one of the most effective stress buster. And fortuitously, era can help us to reduce the hours we spend meditating, with the equal stress-lowering gain a monk could likely get.

You might need to save round for a chunk of technology referred to as binaural beats. Research has proven that using binaural beats for 20 mins a day is equal to hours of meditation. I use a enterprise known as Profound Meditation and can pretty advise them.

Another super manner to reduce pressure is to in reality exercising. I'm not speakme about walking, weight lifting and unique sweaty-tough-to-do physical activities proper proper here. Merely strolling for half-hour a day will do wonders for your temper.

Thesestrain busters will do extra for you than pillow beating, shouting, or maybe leaping off a aircraft. (with a parachute of direction) I do them ordinary.

I do not expect I want to remind you of all the blessings of pressure bargain. Aside from being a higher learner, you're more likely to make friends with a smiling face. Rather than a scowling or a "zombie" face.

So now that you've located a manner to reduce pressure shall we skip directly to the following concern remember. How to focus on boring and dry courses.

How to Study Boring Subjects

Lets face it, reading is a chore once in a while. Sure, you will in all likelihood love records because of that cute professor, however not all professors are adorable. So how do you awareness and ace your uninteresting concern? It's much less complicated than you trust you studied. Let's get started out.

First of all, it's been tested that humans can not recognition on a humdrum scenario for an prolonged term. Research has proven that we will most effective awareness on a humdrum scenario for approximately 20 mins in advance than our thoughts starts offevolved wandering and final down.

So if you pressure your self to look at for added than 20 mins then you definately're just losing it sluggish. This would not propose that you do not have a take a look at for extra than 20 mins an afternoon. It certainly manner that you need to rest in among 20 mins periods.

For example, here's a schedule that I often use:

•Study for 20 mins

•Take a five minute smash

•Continue to have a take a look at for 20 mins

•Take a 5 minute wreck

•Continue to observe for 20 minutes

•Repeat the above steps for one greater time. In unique terms you'll look at for a complete of two hours, now not counting the five minute breaks.

•Rest for half of-hour after 2 hours of reading.

•Study for two greater hours earlier than calling it a day.

It may additionally moreover appear that 4 hours of reading regular with day is barely enough but take delivery of as actual with me its loads, if you recognition with a laser-like intensity. Haruki Murakami, the worldwide acclaimed and bestseller writer, claimed an top notch way to art work for best five to 6 hours a day. And this is best after years of sharpening his awareness and artwork ethic.

So what do I recommend through laser-like attention and the way do you acquire it? By laser-like recognition I imply: the functionality to attention on your work without getting distracted. It's absolutely you and your paper, or your pc's display display screen.

Laser Focus Technique

How to awareness like a laser is a superb deal extra hard to provide an purpose at the back of however I've simplified it and made it smooth for you.

First, you could increase your attention thru predicting on the same time as your 20 minutes of analyzing block will prevent.

So get a stopwatch and set a 20 mins countdown timer. Once you've got carried out that, dive into your books and begin analyzing. Once in a while, try to are looking ahead to how heaps time is left considering the truth which you have started out. For a few bizarre reason, this may refocus your interest on your books or paper. Don't fear in case you overlook to do this, as this shows you are too focused to even do not forget.

The Einstein Focus Method

Here's each different trick you could strive. Albert Einstein trained himself his interest the usage of this very approach. Here's how Einstein does it: Every time you're distracted.

Except whilst you are attempting to expect the time left for your 20 minutes block.

Write down "I will no longer be distracted on this way all yet again" on a clean piece of paper. Proceed to write down down down the perfect terms every time you're distracted.

After some time your unconscious will begin to get the idea and forestall distracting you with every snicker, snorts, and farts out of your classmates' orifice. Important as they'll be.

OK, now that we realize the way to interest and the way to reduce your stress degree, we need to popularity on task management. Most of the famous technique in challenge management are too complicated for college youngsters. They are a waste of time and you in all likelihood may not be able to maintain a complex gadget except. (no offense, I, too, can't preserve complicated systems)

However a clean to do list is simply too smooth. That's why I virtually have a way called the Flow List.

Flow List

The Flow List is in fact a to do list with a very critical twist. First, you want to put together a small pocket ebook, it want to be small sufficient that you may wholesome it into your pocket. No, you can not use a clever cellular phone for the Flow List.

There's a completely important cause why you purchased to do this with a pen and paper. The purpose is due to the truth we procrastinate on matters that our subconscious mind could now not assume is important. And the excellent manner to make our unconscious mind understand what's vital is to in reality remind it, over and over all over again. If this is complex, don't worry you may recognize this in reality in a 2d.

So right right here's what you do, after you've got were given your pen and a small pocket book, write your to do listing at the number one internet net web page. Never write more than one internet web page of to-dos. If you've got got were given greater to-dos then it is too lousy because of the reality you're no longer going to write down them down. Now start doing all your duties and go out any to-dos which you've finished.

And then on day after today you ought to check any brilliant to-dos and transfer them to a cutting-edge internet page. Do this for every single awesome to-dos devices. Every time you fail to scratch off your first rate to-dos objects and have to write them again and again over again, your unconscious gets an increasing number of hectic for you to complete it. To in the end scratch it off the rattling listing.

The Flow List is a very effective manner to get subjects finished so strive it for as a minimum 30 days. You can use it for anything, simply.

From the subsequent monetary damage on-wards, the strategies provided may be extra complex and harder to do. I've made it as smooth and clean as feasible for you. However, there can be only a lot I can do to simplify it. As Einstein stated, make it smooth but now not too simple.

The correct facts is, the strategies within the following few chapters have to honestly accelerate your reading pace and comprehension. They are the "gem stones" and "ruby" of my mystery stack of studying systems. They are what made me into who I am nowadays. A learning prodigy on steroids.

Chapter 5: The Feynman Method

It might now not rely how stunning your principle is, it does not rely how clever you are. If it'd not don't forget test, it is inaccurate.

- Richard Feynman

OK, we have included quite a few cloth so we may want to do a recap:

•Speed listening is quicker than pace reading.

•Always pace pay hobby whenever you have were given got a down-time. I.E. Going for a jog.

•Your notes want to embody massive mind, elements, definitions and huge questions. This is for non-technical courses first-rate

•Your notes, for technical guides, have to exceptional encompass "elements" and occasionally "definitions".

•use TreeDBNotes to your non-technical guides. Pen and paper for technical publications.

•pressure prevents learning - the fine way to lessen strain is to meditate using binaural beats and exercising.

•Study in 20 mins block.

•Use the "laser interest method" and the "Einstein technique" to attention on your studies. The former technique consists of seeking to "wager" how an lousy lot time is left on your 20 mins block of time. The latter technique includes writing down the sentence "i won't be distracted through manner of this once more", every time you get distracted.

•Utilize the Flow List to warfare procrastination with the assist of your subconscious mind.

So in summary, you currently realise the manner to eat statistics speedy, take notes, and manipulate it slow.

However, ingesting statistics at a breakneck pace could not advise that you'll preserve in mind or apprehend the statistics. This is what this financial disaster is ready.

The Feynman technique is called after a physicist named Richard Feynman. We've prolonged beyond through his listing of achievements inside the Prologue financial disaster. Now we are going to examine how Mr Feynman is able to research and apprehend at a breakneck tempo.

Part of the reason why geniuses or A students may not want to study a bargain to achieve first magnificence is because of the fact they emphasized on information the fabric, an lousy lot extra than rote gaining knowledge of or memorization.

A genius, be definition, doesn't need party pointers just like the reminiscence palace. They don't forget due to the fact they recognize the material. It's like driving a bicycle, as soon asa way to journey a bicycle you in no way forget about.

If you understood the idea of gravity and the way it surely works, you will most likely undergo in thoughts it. With that said, allow's flow into on to the Feynman Method.

With the Feynman method you understand complicated concept or concept thru the usage of pretending that you're going to provide an reason for and/or teach the idea to a child. The splendid way to do this is to draw out the concept and rewrite the jargons into easy terms.

Here are the steps:

1. Choose a idea or idea which you had a difficult time records.

2. Imagine you'll train the concept to a toddler.

three. Write down the concept in easy words and draw when you have to.

4. Ask yourself if the kid will apprehend.

Example:

Let's say I recognize no longer some thing approximately computer systems and would love to discover about the distinction among an IPS display and a ordinary show.

And let's imagine that I've discovered the reason for the IPS display on Wikipedia. It's whole of technical rationalization that I do not apprehend, so I imagined myself schooling it to a ten 12 months antique baby.

Here's the purpose from Wikipedia: "IPS screen stands for In-Plane Switching show and it allows whole shade saturation even when the viewing perspective is not at once within the front of the display display display screen."

Phew, that is difficult to understand and its complete of jargons.

To train that to a ten yr old, I may additionally write some element like "You recognize how is it which you want to sit down right away in the the front of the TV, on the way to reduce glare? With the IPS show you could sit anywhere you want on the sofa and it'd now not count range. There might not be any glare. It could be just like sitting without delay in the the front of the TV"

I may also draw a screen that has a washed out coloration and a human head staring at it from the side in region of the the front. And I may additionally need to draw the IPS display screen showing vibrant shades despite the fact that a human head is looking at it from the facet.

Of path, you'll want to find out the definition of the jargons you do not understand. If I haven't any concept what "full colour saturation" manner, I may additionally in no manner be able to deliver an reason for the IPS show' idea in clean phrases.

The Feynman technique basically forces you to recognize a idea so sincerely, that it's miles truely etched into your mind. It is also useful, as a take a look at on whether you had in fact understood a concept. If you can't train it to a person else the usage of clean words, then you have not definitely grasped the concept. With this, you may never be stuck unprepared and in no way over-confident on exam days.

Troubleshooting

The Feynman approach is not a clean approach like all the specific techniques in preceding chapters. It requires a chunk bit more time and dedication. However, you will be amazed by way of the use of what you can do in a totally quick amount of time.

It might also seem that you're making slow or no development in any respect however the truth is, data some thing calls for some time. Letting the data simmer into facts.

Sometimes you'll likely have some hassle visualizing an photograph to attract and that is awesome too. Not all troubles have an photograph linked to it. An rationalization the use of simple terms will be enough in this case. However, do not get lazy and in fact pass the drawing section.

Chapter 6: How to Remember Everything Without Rote Learning

Memory is not data; idiots can via rote repeat volumes. Yet what's information without memory?

- Tupper, Martin

The capacity to recollect the entirety with out rote gaining knowledge of or repetition studying is probably each pupil's moist dream. No marvel right here, as university students' workload getting increasingly more unmanageable each new semester. Not to say all of the dates we ought to pass, the ever important social existence, the frat occasions, and all the super TV and films. Hey, we've handiest got one shot at this factor called existence, don't we?

So how do you bear in mind all of the facts you want to keep in mind? (In order to pass the exam or get the machine advertising) Before we get into the method themselves, let me explain why I refuse to look at memory techniques like the memory palace.

Memory palace is basically a reminiscence trick, it makes use of your familiarity with the gadgets in your immediate surroundings and peg it to unfamiliar records. For example, you may peg a grocery list (surprising) on every sections of your property. (familiar)

So you peg a banana, as an instance, to the TV. And milk at the sofa, and so forth. It won't be tedious when you have a constrained set of things to keep in thoughts, but it'll get very complicated when you have a couple of set of factors to take into account.

For example, a listing of records, pegged to the entirety on your living room, a few other one pegged on your bed room, and a few extraordinary listing pegged to, probably, your vehicle, the capabilities of your cat likely? Your boyfriends competencies? Ugh.

Don't get me incorrect. The reminiscence palace or peg system is a incredible invention and I may additionally additionally just use it in the destiny. If a person can discover the way to do it in a greater realistic manner. Not to say humane.

You see, the peg tool became invented by using way of the Greeks to memorize one debate. After the talk is over they used the equal familiar room for some other debate. It isn't always intended for multiple units of statistics, technical terms and in reality no longer for teachers. The Greeks are well-known for voluntarily torturing themselves besides. Trust me, stay faraway from the Greeks!

There are better ways.

Such as taking gain of what present day-day scientists has uncovered about how the memory works and a way to optimize it. You see, the brilliant way to research is to use your visible and auditory capability.

What do I endorse by means of manner of that? It's easy. Academic studying is largely approximately visual mastering. Audio analyzing is less so, however however vital. Don't accept as true with me?

Let me ask you this. When have become the remaining time you had dissected a frog? And how a outstanding deal time does realistic, hands on route gets allotted in a mean semester? Unless you're studying to be a mechanic, you don't get to do much at the aspect of your palms at all. So you do not study an entire lot out of your enjoy of touch.

You do now not examine thousands out of your experience of fragrance and flavor too. This is pretty self explanatory.

So what approximately the visible experience? You use it nearly all of the time, every outside and inside the study room. If you're studying a textbook then definately definately're the usage of your eyes to check the symbols on the net net web page called phrases, and you use your auditory experience whilst you repeat the phrases on your head.

Sure, you use auditory masses too, whilst you're within the class and the professor is yapping non-prevent. However, maximum of the time, your professor organized diagrams, charts, strength factors, and test aids, too. Plus, you're actively visualizing what the professor is speaking approximately. Yes, visualization or forming a picture in your mind's eye is taken into consideration seen as properly.

The brilliant students, therefore, are normally dominant of their visible revel in. This method that they'll be better at the usage of their visual experience than all in their different experience. They check better the use of seen than, say, with auditory.

This is a result of a bias in how the instructional international pick out to disseminate statistics. It's a stark contrast with the apprentice model of preceding age.

Unfortunately, there can be nearly not anything you could do to alternate this device. If you are not predominantly visible, you want to discover ways to use your seen functionality (tremendous, you have one and I will show it to you) more correctly.

Don't take shipping of as true with me that the incredible college college students, even geniuses, are predominantly visual? Let me ask you, what is the epitome of a excellent pupil? My bet would be the handiest which can eat, remember and apprehend records quicker and higher than everyone else.

And what's a genius (in studying and knowledge speed) however a human with photographic reminiscence? A student with photographic memory can, not most effective, eat and recall facts quicker than all people else but is familiar with the facts higher than anyone else.

This is because of the truth know-how a chunk of records is predicated carefully in your current knowledge. Let me provide you with an instance, if I let you know that your coronary coronary coronary heart works like a pump however you have got in no way visible a pump in advance than, you could no longer understand me. However, in case you've visible a pump and recognize the way it works then you may apprehend how a coronary coronary coronary heart works immediately.

Our Associative Brain

You see, our mind is an associative machine. A toddler is conscious and learns with the aid of associating phrases with bodily items. For example, parents will frequently teach their kids via pronouncing a word out loud, say "desk", and then pointing to a real desk.

The baby's thoughts now links the sound "table" with a real desk. We study the whole lot with the useful resource of affiliation. Children learns that touching a boiling pot of water is not a wonderful concept via manner of the use of affiliation.

At first he does no longer recognize what being burned seems like, till he touches a boiling pot. The ache is right away and the mind partner the boiling pot with the ache right now.

So if you have a photographic memory and likes to look at, you'll have an first-rate capability to understand new idea faster than a everyday guy.

Let me provide you with some other instance. Computer programming languages are tedious to research for maximum people. This is due to the truth programming commands like "href", as an example, is bizarre and remote places to most people. We do now not realize what it manner and our thoughts has no concept what "href" is associated with.

However, in case you've found out that "href" genuinely way "to link" in Latin, then it'd be a piece of cake to recollect the command "href". This is truly an instance, I have no idea what "href" simply approach.

What This Means For You

By now, you need to comprehend how important the visible revel in is to getting to know a few component fast. That's how books, motion pix, instructions and trainings are created. They are created to be fed on visually and by way of the use of way of auditory.

And there is an splendid motive for that, human beings are predominantly seen beings. Up to 50% of our mind is dedicated to the processing seen pix and actions.

You may also additionally scoff on the declaration above, brushing off it via pronouncing that you can't even visualize, or which you do now not have a mind's eye. Let me display it to you which you're no longer first-class very seen however you are quite right at visualizing stuff.

If your dad and mom stroll through the door of your lecture hall in the destiny, ought to you be capable of understand them? If you could, then you definitely have the capacity to visualize. For what's visualization if no longer the photograph to your head? And what is reputation, if no longer the way of matching what you note in the real international with the image for your head? It's definitely no longer feasible to apprehend some issue without the capability to visualise.

Visualization is surely the way of creating a photograph or an photo to your head. Try this. Think of the word "Imagine" and attempt to project it right into a easy wall. So the wall will now have the word "don't forget" written all through it. Now, attempt to make it purple. And then trade the phrase into green, red and yellow.

If you could do this, you could visualize. However, you may now not have a robust, sharp, and colourful picture on your mind's eye but.

Thus, all the techniques on this financial disaster is dedicated to sharpen your seen processing abilties. But earlier than we keep, shall we do a recap.

•The educational gadget is set up in a manner to frequently gain the visible novices.

•Auditory sense is used an awful lot a great deal less often than seen.

•A reading genius is someone with a exceptional seen capability.

•Our mind knows and recollects via associating portions of data with gift quantities of information.

•50% to eighty% of the processing electricity in our thoughts is devoted to the visible experience on my own.

 OK, we should go with the flow at once to the subsequent financial disaster, in which we will talk about the motive why we neglect about about.

Chapter 7: Why We Forget

No guy has an top notch sufficient memory to be a a hit liar.

- Abraham Lincoln

I apprehend you might be lack of existence to leap ahead to the reminiscence strategies however do no longer do that. It's vital that you understand why and the manner we neglect topics first. Trust me, it isn't always because you have got were given a awful reminiscence.

We already understand that the visible sense is paramount to acquire excessive grades to your studies. And we already recognise that we're capable of without issues recognize a foreign places concept, if we have were given were given an gift piece of facts this is applicable to the foreign idea.

There's a few other motive why gaining knowledge of is so tough for optimum humans. It has to do with the cause why it is so hard to preserve in mind humans's name.

You see, human beings's name may be very easy to bear in mind, if you realize how. It's hard to remember due to the fact you were not paying interest and there may be no pre-present information to latch the call onto.

Let me provide an motive for.

How tough is it to overlook approximately the call "smith"? It's pretty clean to don't forget, right? How about Joe? It is at the same time as we're faced with names like Mikalski that we overlook approximately.

First, we're now not in all likelihood to have an gift database of the decision Mikalski so it's miles tougher to insert it into our mind's cell. And how do you even spell it? With a name like Joe, we can without a doubt see the word JOE in our thoughts's eye. And subsequently, we in reality do not pay sufficient interest.

You see, reminiscence is regularly idea as the potential to do not forget or retrieve a certain facts from our thoughts. That's proper but incomplete. There's now not some thing wrong together along with your functionality to retrieve a positive facts from your mind. In fact, your functionality to remember is probably amazingly suitable. The hassle lies with the manner you spot the area.

The police force has prolonged seemed that eye witness' account can in fact range from one man or woman to each other. Eye witnesses regularly gave conflicting facts to the police. A witness may also moreover document that the assassin turned into wearing a red blouse. Another also can moreover say that the murderer changed into, in fact, sporting a blue hooded T-shirt. It seems that humans's hold in mind of latest memory is faulty at tremendous.

However, the fact is that the attention witnesses' critiques are regularly correct and proper. How can this be?

This is due to the reality they sincerely did undergo in thoughts precisely what they noticed. I understand this is puzzling however live with me right proper here. You see, the gadgets round us does no longer flows into our eyes and our mind unfiltered. The way that you apprehend the arena isn't similar to how I recognize it. It's like seeing the sector thru filtered glasses.

Here's how our eyes art work. The items round us shows lighting fixtures into our eyes and electric indicators is sent from the eyes to the brain. Our brain then techniques the electric signs and forms a image. However, we do no longer consciously see every little element spherical us, all the time.

Think of your family. You must have seen their faces thousands of times. Yet, are you in a position to inform me what number of wrinkles they have? Or the locations in their moles?

So what do eye witnesses do even as they'll be pressed for info they did no longer see? Their mind receives modern and begin making subjects up.

Thus, in case your belief is incomplete, your preserve in thoughts is probably defective as nicely.

Chapter 8: The Matrix System

The answer is offered, Neo, and it is searching out you, and it will find out you if you want it to.

- Trinity in The Matrix

I preference you're not overwhelmed thru manner of the exceptional quantity of statistics I dumped on you inside the last 2 chapters.

It's always an awesome idea to do an define so proper right right here is going:

•We keep in mind pictures which is probably clear and sharp.

•We understand records by using way of its dating with one of a kind informations.

That's it!

Now that we realise the way to don't forget and apprehend facts, the solution is pretty sincere. I call it The Matrix because of the truth you are surely "downloading" the statistics into your mind:

1. Chunk down statistics till you can constitute it with a photo.

2. Draw or visualize the image. I.E. Feynman approach

3. Make positive the picture is sharp and easy.

four. Link the facts with contemporary knowledge.

#1. Chunking Down

Information chunking isn't always new. What's new in my technique is how I bite it down. Most human beings will bite down facts with the aid of chapters, sections or mind. This is not maximum gratifying.

An information chew, in step with my non-public definition, is a set of terms that can be represented through an photo. Two associated pix might be first-rate but it simply is the most I could probably skip for. What do I suggest thru this? Here's an example of an facts chunk that has multiple notable photos.

"The best manner to have a examine is to teach others and drop instructions that has a lousy trainer."

In the example above, you have were givenvery distinct photograph of you coaching some other individual, and a have a look at room putting with a awful professor. Of route, your picture also can vary from mine and this is OK. The element is is that we've got got had been givenvery awesome images from the example above.

An most suitable statistics bite might be:

"Use time periods to test."

"Repeat the whole thing you've got heard to your personal voice to in addition cement the facts into your thoughts."

Notice that the two instance above could only produce one orassociated pix. The 2d instance may want to probable produce an photo of your self whispering to your self and the photo of the statistics cementing to your mind. This is top notch as the two pix are very associated with each other and might even permit you to keep the statistics.

This is a very effective technique that does not get used sufficient. Most folks blaze through our readings without a effort to manner the phrases on the net internet web page right into a coherent and crystal smooth pix. Do you recognise that, according to research, we endure in thoughts or apprehend a photo ninety nine.Ninety 9% of the time?

That's tremendous, because we forget eighty% of what we have discovered inside the first 24 hours?

#2. Visualizing or Drawing

The 2nd step is to definitely visualize or draw out the statistics chunk which you want to endure in thoughts.

This is easy due to the truth you have already chunked down a wall of textual content into digestible bits of data. Lets say you want to remember that we forget about eighty% of what we discovered out in only 24 hours.

You want to be capable of visualize a human skull with phrases and equations flying out of her thoughts and the phrase "24 hours" on top of her head. That'srelated pics.

This applies to everything you're seeking to memorize, even jargons. For instance, we could say you are searching for to memorize the jargon "polycarbonate".

Just create an photograph of the word polycarbonate and flash it inside the the front of you. You can challenge it at the wall or any flat ground. You can manipulate the photo too. Make it bold, italics, purple, blue, massive, and and so on.

You might also additionally even separate the word into some chunks. For example, poly carbo nate. It's a excellent deal less complicated to consider and visualize poly, carbo and nate in preference to polycarbonate.

This has to do with the fact that our mind can not hold greater than 7 bits of records at one time. (It's capability however you want schooling) Which is why cellphone numbers are 7 digits, and eight digits now that they have run out of numbers.

As an advantage, say the phrases that you're visualizing out loud. Or whisper it to yourself. This improves undergo in mind later inside the exam because of the fact we are skilled to "voice-out" words at the same time as we look at.

#three. Sharp and Clear

 Once you have got an photo orfor your mind's eye, you must now make sure the picture is plain. An dubious picture has a blurry experience to it. Here's a manner to make it clearer.

1. Apply colours to sharpen and evaluation the images. For instance, you could have phrase images in ambitious and crimson on a white ancient beyond.

2. Apply greater shades.

3. Search for pix on Google if you cannot get a clean photograph.

4. Make wonderful the strains are sharp and darkish if feasible.

#4. Linking

After you have got made first-class your images are flawlessly easy and top notch, you want to now link it to an contemporary-day body of information. Using the "polycarbonate" example above, I may want to link it to the Samsonite difficult cowl baggage.

This very last step is crucial due to the reality our mind is conscious and remembers with the resource of filing a new piece of statistics into present day-day "folders" or neurons.

This is likewise wherein the Feynman approach comes in. I ought to now be able to educate what a polycarbonate is to a 10 12 months antique teenager. I would possibly probable write a few component like "Polycarbonate is a tough, tough but mild plastic used on well-known bags like Samsonite. This is to guard the stuff inside the bags in order that it would not damage."

Of course, what you link Polycarbonate to is probably very particular from my example above. This is because of the fact your modern body of statistics can be unique from me. Or they may be the identical, each way it's far OK, as long as you can keep in thoughts the statistics.

Using The Matrix On Technical Courses

If you want to memorize mathematical equations with the Matrix, definitely do it like the way you memorize a jargon. First, chunk the equations into elements

Example: The device for trapezoid is h/2 (b1 + b2)

Chunk it proper right down to:

Trapezoid =

H/2

(b1 + b2)

Theequation chunks need to be trouble through facet (but in addition aside), of route. And you can make H/2 bold and pink to in addition cement in into your reminiscence, as an example.

Practicing The Matrix System

 Now, this isn't a magic bullet. It may be truly effective if you exercise is diligently but possibilities are you can pass doing the steps above, greater frequently that not. And it's far OK. To be honest, I almost did not include The Matrix System on this ebook because of its tedious nature. However, the advantages overshadowed the try required.

My recommendation? Take it slow, at the least for the primary month. The satisfactory way to construct a dependancy is to take small consistent steps that slightly takes any time and effort. For instance, create absolutely one records chunk consistent with day to visualize. Or perhaps even definitely growing an records bite and prevent right there.

The key's to be constant about it and do it regular.

Also, when you have trouble visualizing regardless of what you do, here's a tip. Try looking up towards your brow, your left brow and your right forehead. Find an area that permits you to form the clearest photo. You'll be surprised how effective this smooth trick is.

The information supplied in this economic destroy is more effective that you in all likelihood recognize. This is the foundation of the wonderful memory guides on hand, along with some photographic reminiscence training publications.

Armed with this information, you may test anything you need, even physical competencies like martial arts. (The key is to visualize the kind of scenario wherein you'll use a extremely good punching or kicking actions as you practice) Other advantages encompass Alzheimer's prevention, and maintaining your thoughts "plastic". (Learning stuff fast like a baby even in advanced age.)

After you've got constructed a addiction spherical The Matrix System, you is probably annoyed with the lack of readability on your photograph. Don't fear, we're able to deal with the issue in the subsequent chapter.

Chapter 9: Matrix Streaming

If real is what you can feel, odor, taste and study, then 'real' is in reality electric powered powered indicators interpreted thru your mind.

- Morpheus in The Matrix

OK, on this bankruptcy we are going to talk approximately the manner to bolster your visualization's muscle. Yes, absolutely absolutely everyone can visualize as we've covered in previous monetary smash, but no longer certainly all and sundry can visualize vibrant and clear snap shots.

That's why the sports activities in this economic catastrophe is designed to boost your visualization muscle. The bodily sports activities are every clean and easy to do. The trick, once more, is to do it everyday.

The first workout is referred to as the Matrix Streaming workout and the concept is quite easy. You draw out the energy of your visualization from inside you after which materialize it with the aid of describing it.

Here's the way it genuinely works.

1. Prepare a recorder, it can be your clever cell phone, pc, laptops and and many others. As extended as it has the functionality to report your voice.

2. discover 20 minutes (at the minimum) regular for this workout. If you're uncomfortable with human beings listening to your innermost mind, then you definitely definately ought to discover a quiet region to try this.

3. Sit down resultseasily

4. Think of a hassle or a question that frustrates you and ask yourself "What is the answer to hassle X?"

5. Alternatively, you may truely sit down down and wait.

6. When you've got finished one of thestep above, pay very close interest to any snap shots that pops out on your head.

7. You will short observe that your inner thoughts is continuously shooting up pix.

8. Now, start describing every pix that pops up to your head in vibrant statistics. For instance, I see a pink coloured residence with a big cherry wood door. It's surrounded via manner of white timber fences and has a manicured, inexperienced garden. It also has...and lots of others and many others.

nine. Please remember to file down your descriptions of the pix.

 That's it! This simple exercising, like all of the ones we have got were given talked about before this, is incredibly clean however very effective in strengthening your visualization talent.

However, you could stumble upon some issues even as you try to describe the pictures that pops up in your head. The topics is, sometimes your vocabulary is probably inadequate. Or the image is so blurry that you cannot make sense of it.

If you are lacking the important vocabulary, you will possibly need to make use of the dictionary and glossary. However, do now not prevent midway on the equal time as you're doing the Matrix Streaming. Plow on thru explaining in preference to describing.

For example, if you're trying to mention "jelly fish" however you are momentarily out of place for phrases, then you may say some aspect like "a shape of sea creature with a translucent thoughts and stingers sticking out of it's miles brain."

If your photo is blurry, truely stay up for it to sharpen or sit up for a few other photo to pop up, replacing the blurry image.

The reality is, in case you're having quite a few hassle doing the Matrix Streaming workout then it might have some factor to do with spelling bee. Let me offer an reason at the back of.

On a ordinary spelling bee exam in the course of the u . S . A ., there is probably most effective one ethnic enterprise with extremely good grades. The Asians are quite actual in memorizing spellings. For a while, this burdened researches. The Asians are generally more hardworking, sure, but this does not offer an reason for the distance with further hardworking university college students from one-of-a-kind ethnic institution.

Also, endure in thoughts that the ones Asians that I'm talking approximately are born and raised inside the United States. They ate similar meals, raised in similar surroundings, and had get entry to to the entirety an American pupil has in favored. So what's the distinction? Turns out the difference is TV.

You see, Asian dad and mom protects their kids from the TV almost viciously. There's no TV in advance than homework, training, and further readings is completed. And even then, there is top notch 1 to 2 hours of TV time allotted consistent with day.

It's the identical form of affiliation and time allotment for laptop video video games and browsing the Internet. If they'll be allowed to in any respect. Now, some parents may never do that to their children. In fact, a whole lot of dad and mom might possibly see that as a sort of abuse. And I don't have any doubt that you is probably enraged, as a baby, if your parents had barred you from TV, video video video games and the Internet.

Turns out, with out a TV, pc video video games, and the Internet, Asian youngsters are compelled to visualise extra than their counterpart. How so? First of all, its extraordinarily stupid without those modern leisure devices so the ones Asian youngsters entertain themselves with "myth video video games" like dolls, bodily toys, and and plenty of others.

Secondly, Asian kids in fact take a look at more short testimonies. Again, due to the truth there can be truly no one of a kind shape of entertainments. This has the effect of strengthening their visualization's muscle considerably at a very more youthful age. This is due to the reality you can not experience a e-book with out visualizing a "movie" from phrases.

In precis, you need to watch manner masses less TV than you are right now, and you ought to read manner more books. Fiction books like Harry Potter is first rate for boosting your visualization capabilities.

Now, The Matrix Streaming method has a number of advantages related to it. If you do it for some months constantly, you will start noticing that you are more innovative, your memory improves and you examine quicker. Focusing on visualization is that crucial to your lifestyles.

Chapter 10: Zero Hour & Keystone Habit

We are what we again and again do. Excellence, then, is not an act, but a addiction.

- Aristotle

In 1999 Naperville's college college students took the TIMSS (Trends in International Mathematics and Science Study) test and accomplished the scores of 6th in mathematics and 1st in technological expertise. This is amongst 230,000 university university college students from all around the worldwide, along with heavyweight (in technological understanding and math) like Singapore and Japan.

This success is in sharp comparison to falling grades of colleges all around the america, particularly inside the area of technological know-how and arithmetic. So what did Napperville did that makes them so a success? We'll communicate approximately that in a 2nd, however first we should take a look at some distinct weird phenomena.

Willpower and actual conduct are hard to shape. Everybody is aware of that what you're speculated to do as a way to gain goal X. For instance, you're purported to devour an awful lot much less in case you want to get thin. However, many did not adhere to even smooth instructions. And it's miles not due to the reality they do now not need to be slender, wealthy, or famous. In many times, they're determined to gain their reason.

It's antique statistics that new twelve months's resolutions, more frequently that not, fail to bring about alternate every twelve months, and however it's far although one of the most famous time of the 365 days to set goals. What's now not apparent is the fact that humans fail to trade or obtain their reason most of the time, regardless of what time of the yr it's miles.

So while a group of humans, who had failed at nearly every hard goal they've got ever set their eyes on, overhauled their whole lives, the research drew a hurricane of hobby.

Some researchers and scientists are so skeptical of the end cease result that they attempted to disprove it with the aid of manner of designing the identical test.

The result? Each and every one of the participant's lives superior and new behavior were commonplace. The participant started attaining their dreams and the entirety in their lives advanced. They start smoking much less, workout greater, had extra difficulty and so on.

So what does Napperville's college students has to do with the trouble in the test above? Nothing hundreds it appears, besides for one key similarities. The scientists calls it the Keystone Habit and Napperville's trainer calls it the Zero Hour.

Zero Hour & Keystone Habit

 So what is the Zero Hour and Keystone Habit that modified the lives of students and research player? It's workout. You see, Zero Hour refers back to the hour before first period starts offevolved offevolved at Nashville college and it is a period wherein college college students exercised tough. Everyone is wanted to achieve at the least eighty% of their maximum coronary coronary coronary heart charge.

The Keystone Habit studies participant? They are required to popularity at the exercise dependancy and not some thing else. The enhancements of their lives are without a doubt "element consequences" from taking on an exercise regime.

This is a traditional, 80/20 law at play. If you do no longer already recognize, the eighty/20 regulation is the regulation that is first placed with the useful resource of an Italian economist named Wilfredo Pareto. So sometimes the 80/20 regulation is referred to as the Pareto regulation. The law states that eighty% of the results or output is generally produced by using the use of 20% of the input or strive. This virtually approach plenty much less is greater or do loads less and get more.

The trick is finding out the 20% of the enter that produces 80% of the quit end result.

The Pareto regulation has lengthy been examined to be actual. It's everywhere. In the economic system, earnings branch of a business enterprise, in the lawn, and and so on.

80/20 Law of Academic Success

Exercise in this situation isn't in truth an eighty/20 law but furthermore a serves a waterfall impact. Let me explain. If the eighty/20 law offers you out-sized consequences for little strive then the Waterfall effect offers you an out-sized results for each area of your life for little or no try.

Exercise will not satisfactory beautify your instructional end result but offers you extra discipline, fitness, self-discipline, motivation, better cognitive capacity, reduce stress and so forth.

With that stated, allow's skip directly to how you can reap the maximum output with minimum input. Because we could face it, there's only a few individuals who would love to exercising each day for a few hours.

Here's what you have to do as an alternative:

1. Start via on foot 1/2-hour an afternoon if you're now not worth.

2. After strolling for approximately 2 weeks, put together a coronary heart fee screen.

3. Gauge your maximum coronary coronary heart rate with the beneficial useful resource of deducting 220 from your age. For instance, in case you're now 21, your maximum coronary coronary heart charge might be 220 - 21 = 199.

four. Jog and run every day for at least half of-hour, which will gain 70% to eighty% of your maximum coronary coronary heart charge. If your MHR is 199 then you definitely ought to intention for a hundred and sixty beats consistent with minute coronary heart charge at the equal time as you are exercising.

What To Do When You Refuse to Exercise

If you're like me, you hate exercise. And if you are like me, you could not stay with an exercise utility for quite a number of days.

This is regular and want to be expected. However, there's some matters you can do to maximise the threat that you may exercising normal. First of all, you want to put together all your strolling clothes and shoes the night time time before and region them on the element of your mattress, making sure you could step on them whilst you got far from mattress. This tip on my own has doubled my workout fee. I now continually workout, in which I used to procrastinate and had a sporadic exercising agenda.

The 2nd tip is to allow yourself bypass the exercising if you do not feel find out it not possible to resist. The handiest caveat proper right here is that you need to get off your butt and run for 1 minute in advance than you give up on it. Chances are, you may keep on foot.

This tip might be very powerful at destroying any excuses that your unconscious comes up with. Nobody can argue with a one minute exercising, do you have got got somewhere to move inner one minute? Or perhaps you're feeling ill? If so, let's have a look at how ill you actually are with one minute of exercise. Chances are, you're now not as sick as you notion your self to be and the exercise will make you experience higher besides.

Like I stated earlier on this chapter, that could be a keystone dependancy that impacts every regions of your lifestyles. So please do it.

Chapter 11: College And The You Factor

"Top grades don't usually visit the brightest college college students. Knowing the way to make the maximum of your innate talents counts for brought. Infinitely greater."

~ Herbert Walberg ~

Professor of Education at the University of Illinois at Chicago

The Truth approximately College Readiness

College. It's the notable of times. It's the maximum hard of instances. If you're feeling a chunk out of sorts with the academic factors of your college revel in, you are not on my own. Fact is, droves of immoderate university grads make their way onto the campuses of colleges and universities across the region and discover they'll be much less than enthused about assembly the wishes of university life. The time period "unwell-prepared" includes mind.

Suddenly, further to constructing and coping with a colorful social existence (an absolute necessity on this age of consistent connectivity and collaboration), you want to discover a manner to present 100% in your instructional efforts as well. It

can be tough to grasp each the social and the academic factors of the university experience. Knowing when to say at the same time as on either the the front is difficult, especially within the starting. But it's feasible.

To located your thoughts relaxed, I'll will assist you to in on a few exciting factoids about the trap 22 state of affairs lots of your classmates are dealing with. According to ACT, Inc., in 2012, extra than 1.5 million university college students took the ACT. Of that amount, extra than 1 / four of take a look at takers fell quick of meeting college readiness benchmarks for all four most vital test instructions – English, Math, Science and Social Studies.

Even among pinnacle performers, actual grades, a immoderate I.Q. And the capacity to ace standardized exams become not a easy indicator of whether or now not or no longer a student had advanced the expertise set essential to acquire success in university. That's because of the truth frequently the present of intelligence gives a pupil the freedom to coast. Learning comes resultseasily. A scholar who can pick out topics up fast can also have a propensity to depend upon his or her natural skills as opposed to growth appropriate observe behavior, listening skills and a strong art work ethic. Years later, at the same time as the pupil is in the long run faced with the undertaking of reading to research greater complex cloth, she or he famous the potential underdeveloped. At that factor, final a top-performer suddenly requires a chunk ethic the scholar many no longer virtually have, but his or her preceding achievements.

The first step to success in some issue is to recognize yourself. Your academic achievement in college relies upon in your functionality to use a specialised set of abilties.

Take a quick inventory of your middle competencies and be honest. Which of these essential university skills do you presently own? Which of those important university talents do you want to gather?

9 Core Competencies for College Success

∞The ability to arrange and prioritize duties

∞The functionality to control time control successfully

∞The consistency to work incrementally in small chunks

∞Great memorization abilties

∞The ability to look at and look at new necessities (which means after you recognize them, you can sum them up for, say, a more younger sibling or cousin in a single smooth sentence)

∞The capacity to speedy attention and pay interest for as a minimum an hour at a time

∞The functionality to actually and efficiently speak every verbally and in writing

∞The functionality to be responsible to yourself

∞The potential to speak up for yourself (as in, "Hang on, Professor. I don't get that component. Say that again.")

This competencies stock is non-negotiable in terms of your success in university. Without reading maximum of those capabilities, you could not carry out in addition to you could in college.

The fact of the trouble is a person is paying that lets in you to attend college, whether or not or not it's you or your folks. So take the opportunity to max out your capability and get all you could from enjoy. The turn detail of searching for to skate thru is you spend four years chasing your tail. That way masses of overdue night time paper writing, all-day pseudo-reading and wearing around the shame of a laugh at the same time as you need to be reading and analyzing at the same time as you'll rather be enjoyable. Believe it or no longer, it's in reality easier to simply do your fantastic.

What Type of Student Are You?

Watch any college-themed movie and numerous acquainted pupil stereotypes will quickly emerge the geek, the jock, the slacker, the overachiever, the difficult worker and relying on the film rating, the co-ed whose information appears to lie absolutely in his or her dealings with the possibility intercourse. As a depend variety of dependancy, we frequently separate ourselves into commands. The university years are not any precise. Sometimes we do it via choice; from time to time the designation is the stop give up result of enter and barriers positioned on us thru instructors, coaches, parents or others in positions of authority.

One of the keys to success in university (or any other endeavour, for that rely) is self-consciousness. Understanding your strengths and your weaknesses offers you the high-quality gain of being capable of use your innate abilities to fuel your fulfillment. Strength is best strong while you use it. A weakness is handiest

vulnerable factor at the same time as you

misappropriate it as a electricity.

As we skip down the list of the following pupil profiles, I don't want you to do not forget them as everlasting designations. Rather, keep in mind the descriptions as trends you likely very own and testimonies you've had. The fact that your behavior and tales align you with one profile these days doesn't suggest that's wherein you'll live for the duration of your college career. Labels and instructions are a protracted manner lots less crucial than information a way to use your personal assets and reduce the impact of your liabilities. They key proper now can be to begin formulating a way. Successful techniques make right use of the tools and guns you need to your arsenal.

Your modern-day-day profile is your starting point. Look at in which you're. Figure out in which you need to head and permit's make a plan for buying there.

Chapter 12: The Stress Junkie

Motto: "I art work remarkable beneath strain."

Primary strengths: Intensity, intelligence, natural capability

Primary weaknesses: Lack of self-self assurance, driven with the resource of feelings, loss of consciousness

If you're a Stress Junkie, you're a few aspect like an academic twister. You have a propensity to procrastinate and to turn out to be distracted with out problems, and it units you up for a cycle of perpetual fretting, stressing and playing capture-up. You do have the functionality to prepare and put into effect a more effective machine, but you don't do it. You are admittedly intimidated through the concept of normal overall performance and what this type of show of excellence may require from you. You regularly say you parent best beneath stress, but that's now not truly authentic. Very few human beings are at their wonderful while below strain. After all, our fight or flight reflex is designed to be activated at the same time as we find out ourselves in worrying conditions. You bear in mind combat or flight, proper? Gives you tunnel vision, minimizes

creativity and boundaries mind feature till you are out of damage's way. So even as you have made it a dependancy to position your self in traumatic situations, your intrinsic human nature in reality prevents you from appearing your best.

With the threat of different human beings's unmet expectations of you looming, you pick out flight mode over combat mode, which makes you avoid doing all your paintings till the final possible minute. Chances are, you're genuinely quite smart. That's the most effective way you could spend so much time fretting then spend so little time jogging and although make out appropriate sufficient in the long run. If you ever make the selection to harness your electricity, create a protracted-time period success technique and redirect your scattered reputation on task a unmarried intention, you turns into an unstoppable stress.

The Proverbial Slacker

Motto: "No issues."

Primary Strengths: Clarity, recognition, [limited] interest, ease, appearing chops

Primary Weaknesses: Little respect for time, can't see the wooded area for the trees, impaired lengthy-time period vision, performing chops

If you're a proverbial slacker - whether or no longer you're a phony slacker or the actual deal – your claim to reputation is taking it easy. You don't do the work. You don't even hassle drumming up strain on the closing minute to gasoline an all-night time have a have a look at consultation the night time in advance than the huge test. That's not you. You have a perpetual air of disinterest that makes those round you marvel why you ever showing as a whole lot as campus on the first actual day.

The trouble with slackers, but, is the act ultimately wearies, and the actor grows tired of showing as a lot as locations surely to fake his or her presence and input does not count number wide variety. When that happens, you want to spend the following couple of days, weeks, months or years playing capture-up and the entire slacker affair amounts to one large waste of time.

Your capability to tune out and determine to doing the whole lot however what you possibly need to be doing is definitely one among your best strengths. When you turn that electricity proper-facet-up, it's known as hobby, and you've got have been given loads of that. So your number one recourse for killing off this slacker individual is to make a dedication to yourself to attention at the effects you really want to appearance and get to paintings turning in them. Consistently.

The Hard Worker

Motto: "You realize what? I'm gonna pass. I gotta (fill in the blank)."

Primary Strengths: Persistence, paintings ethic, willpower, intensity

Primary weaknesses: Lack of focus, inefficient, exchange-resistant

The Hard Worker is an admirable fella. Kudos to you if you're this man. You paintings difficult, and if you can ever loose up sufficient time, you may probably play hard too. But then free time is the issue, isn't it?

You behavior your affairs with depth, and things are pretty black and white with you. You are continual. You art work at a task till it's done and don't thoughts doing it piece-by using using way of-piece and coming at a problem from all one of a kind angles... as long as you understand, all your unique hassle-solving angles are probable to paintings.

However, it's tough if you want to implement trade. That poses pretty a hassle too due to the fact in phrases of your course load, you spend time; you don't make investments time. The quantity of hours you placed right into a task isn't always proportionate to the results you get out of a project.

I may want to project to mention that your primary hassle is considered one of attention. You spend a whole lot of time at your desk or in the the front of your laptop pretending to artwork. Your motive isn't to fool everybody. You likely enjoy like you are strolling because of your lots-toiling. But toiling isn't just like working. Just just like the use of all your might likely to grip the the the the front bumper of a car isn't just like lifting the automobile. The efforts can also look similar on the outdoor, however the final results can be very specific due to the fact the muscle businesses required to execute a grip are precise from the ones required to execute a boost.

You're gripping, my friend.

Spend less electricity toiling and more energy learning to pay interest and artwork. You will reduce your have a look at time down through at the least half of of and likely pull in better grades extra constantly.

The Guy Who Has It All Figured Out

Motto: "Let me take a look at my time table."

Primary strengths: Self-attention, manage, paintings ethic, commercial enterprise business enterprise

The Guy (or Gal) who has it All Figured Out excels every academically and socially. He is a right now-A scholar and may efficiently keep numerous extraordinary positions like an athlete, chief and social magnet. While his or her grades can be accurate, you don't see this scholar obsessing over grades or spending all day and all night time time time inside the library. There are few subjects extra critical to him than time, control and stability. That's because of the truth he is aware those 3 topics play a massive role in his general achievement and happiness at some point of the ones all-important college years.

The key to carrying out the extent of success this student has attained absolutely is understanding your very very very own abilties and obstacles and knowledge which of your dispositions to maximise and which to restriction. There is not any magic method, only making plans, and execution.

Everyone Learns Differently

Now that we've identified some of your strengths and weaknesses permit's flow in advance and component out the plain: people are extraordinary. So bet what? People analyze in some other manner. That approach what works for a person else in your sphere of impact might not supply the identical effects for you.

If you need to make yourself truly depressing, positioned all of your electricity into trying to be a person else. This is quite probably the worst use of treasured time and valuable resources. It's now not hard to discover your self in a funk while you're preoccupied with what truly everybody else is doing.

Consider this: by the point you reap university, you have were given probably spent a few aspect like 13 years in college being officially informed. The not unusual university day is 7 hours and you attended extra or much less 170 days of college everyday with 12 months for thirteen years. Let's account for the handful of days you're out sick or taking a private day, and you continue to have more than 15,000 days of school beneath your belt in advance than you ever arrive on campus. You should be an expert at university.

And you're.

If you look back over your academic profession, you could recall your successes. You may additionally moreover recall what you possibly did to gain fulfillment while you have got been. You can also moreover keep in mind departing out of your norm and going the extra mile on multiple event.

Do you bear in mind the remaining time you put in late hours wearing out on-line research or worked over a paper that could make the difference among playing sports this season and all at once finding yourself ineligible? You can possibly recollect more than one times wherein you purchased right right here through to your very very very own behalf on the very last minute. The reality is, most folks will make some factor arise while we need to. But it takes the sort of will that is best engaged even as we discover ourselves in dire straits. Willpower will become our emergency reaction. When we're no longer on excessive alert, the emergency reaction isn't delivered approximately, and strength of will is not engaged.

The task you may remedy thru analyzing this ebook is learning to create and rent a gadget of behavior you may depend upon to deliver steady results in the end.

Chapter 13: How the Brain Remembers, How the Brain Forgets

There is not any doubt about it. The human mind is an remarkable piece of system. Its capacity to be in a perpetual country of mastering is the nearest aspect to magic we've were given going. Your mind is continuously at paintings. At any given 2d, it's miles busy remembering, rehearsing, and connecting the dots, developing new thoughts, gathering information, processing stimuli and relaying statistics and instructions to the relaxation of your frame.

Now, earlier than you allow your eyes gloss over and neglect about approximately the following seven-hundred phrases of generation chatter, allow me clarify some thing. My cause in penning this e-book isn't always to give you a listing of things to do and will let you apprehend to purpose them to conduct. My intention is to offer you with a piece of intel that will help you put in force a clean device for becoming a straight away-A pupil.

When it entails training the thoughts to consider some thing, you first need to undergo in thoughts at the same time as you could want to take into account that statistics. Let's say it takes you seconds to examine and recognize a billboard at the educate station. You may not keep in mind this, but if you want to attract near the general cause of the ad, you had to bear in thoughts each phrase you study for a fraction of a 2nd until your thoughts must drift at once to the following phrase and deliver the phrase which means inside the context of the ad itself. Those milliseconds of stored facts are known as without delay recollections.

After studying the advert, you stroll over to the map of train routes published at the wall and decide out the teach you need to adventure is the Red Line north, arriving at 8:forty three AM. The very next train that attracts into the station is the Blue Line train at 8:41 AM. But you recognize that's now not the teach you need. So you wait each different mins and get at the Red Line northbound educate. The statistics you wanted changed into saved in what's called the working reminiscence for only a few minutes. Your thoughts glaringly purges that records out of your strolling memory as quickly because it's been used to make room for introduced facts. Unless you propose on using that train path once more, you can forget about approximately which educate you took and what time it arrived.

Of path, if taking the Red Line teach is part of your every day life, the probabilities are quite correct you can preserve in thoughts the train arrives at eight:forty 3 AM. You received't even ought to look it up another time. In fact, you may additionally apprehend that in case you skip over the Red Line train at eight:forty

3 AM, some extraordinary will come along in 19 mins or so. The statistics you are exposed to time and again and that you hold close immediately to for a while is saved to your lengthy-time period reminiscence.

Your educational success is based carefully on your capacity to build up and keep data in your lengthy-term memory for destiny use. Your university schooling is usually a collection of publications that educate an increasing number of complex requirements yr after three hundred and sixty five days. In order to completely maintain close what you study this year, you have got have been for the reason that permits you to undergo in mind and practice the principles you discovered final 12 months. That manner reading the manner to glide statistics out of your immediately and walking memory in your long-time period memory.

Forgetting is herbal. After analyzing something new, you can forget approximately 1/2 of of of what you determined out inner 24 hours. Remembering is a talent that may be advanced.

Three topics play a big element in how we maintain records: time, the revel in and repetition. Just like in the example, the shorter amount of time you want to maintain in thoughts statistics, the faster your mind will sell off it as quickly because the reminiscence has fulfilled its motive. However, if you need to hang directly to facts a piece longer, the way to do that is by tying the revel in of a surrounding occasion to the reminiscence and rehearsing this connection to your mind time and again earlier than you need to hold in mind it.

The revel in surrounding an event is the "sensory bundle deal deal" that accompanies your reminiscences. We hold in thoughts subjects in chunks. So if there's a specific perfume you need, opportunities are smelling the heady scent will purpose no longer most effective the decision of the fragrance but moreover a string of recollections that make up an revel in which your thoughts has already tied to the smell. You might also bear in mind who wore the fragrance the primary time you smelled it, how the sky appeared that day, what shape of temper you were in and in that you have been whilst you smelled it. That revel in, even though crafted from numerous awesome memories, is woven together to your thoughts and packaged as a unmarried memory.

The truth that you could train your mind to consider way if you make the effort to sharpen your memory, you may probably see large upgrades in your instructional regular standard performance.

7 Tricks For Hanging on to Information

∞Make a conscious selection to take into account. You decide how extended you need a specific memory. Train your mind to do not forget what you are listening to or reading thru identifying what you want to consider and the way you may keep in thoughts it. Create the framework your thoughts needs to keep in mind statistics from the first actual moment you crack open your textbook or pocket e-book.

∞Repetition works wonders for remembering matters. Repetition isn't mumbling a few factor again and again to yourself the night time time time before the check. Repetition is each re-analyzing the records you want to understand or forcing your thoughts to bear in mind the facts you want to recognize over and over over the direction of several weeks.

∞Study or rehearse any new data you've got determined out internal an afternoon or of initial publicity so it doesn't slip away. It's an excellent idea to head over test notes within 48 hours after you're taking them in desire to prepared until check time.

∞Engage your one-of-a-type senses. If you're listening to something that you want to recollect, create to your thoughts a photo to accompany what you are listening to. If you are analyzing, you can maintain in mind records faster if you furthermore repeat key elements aloud.

∞Break information into smaller chunks. Your cellular telephone quantity is 10 digits lengthy but on the same time as you deliver it to someone – whether or not or now not you speak it or write it down – you obviously organization numbers collectively to differentiate among your vicinity code, the primary 3 digits of your cellphone range and the last 4 digits of your wide variety. This way, which we do routinely, is a memory trick.

∞Leverage time. Cramming is like reading a direction map to find out the right train – you nice recollect the facts for a totally quick time. As quick as that take a look at is over, your crowded thoughts will take away extra information from your operating memory to make room for additonal information. Rehearse records repeatedly over the path of days or maybe weeks to shift it from your strolling memory in your lengthy-term reminiscence.

∞When studying for a test, typically skip for ideas. It's tough to don't forget a string of seemingly beside the point data. The thoughts likes to categorize facts in advance than it's saved. If you really need to understand the importance of statistics, apprehend the underlying ideas.

Stop Unrealistic Practices

I'll admit in scripting this e-book; I look at the various books that would line the virtual bookshelf next to this one, and I sincerely have to mention I'm now not completely bought on the advice a few so-known as specialists provide. I would love to have a test the numerous extra famous recommendations you may find in a number of the opposite books and permit you to know why they gained't artwork.

Study Myth #1: Don't observe late at night time

I've heard it stated that scholars shouldn't hit the books overdue at night. Instead, college university students – university university students, no doubt – should hit the books first trouble within the morning. The fact is it doesn't rely what the outdoor clock says. It's extra approximately what your inner clock says.

Ideally, you need to area yourself in a function in that you're analyzing if you have the energy to focus at the concern rely available. That technique every time you're at your exquisite - whether or not or not that's after morning coffee or after Jimmy Kimmel – that's even as you hit the books.

Study Myth #2: Have a hard and speedy examine time. Make a agenda and stick with it.

The lifestyles of a university student is one that calls for a extremely good maintain close to on one of the existence's most treasured abilities – the capacity to charge range it sluggish and electricity. I like the usage of the phrase fee variety with regards to reading due to the fact we recognize the importance of budgeting because it relates to rate variety. Well, permit me let you know. Your time is a much extra valuable resource than coins. Just like you need to have enough coins to cover your economic duties, you're going to need to allocate sufficient time to cover each of your instructional responsibilities. Some subjects would require extra of a time funding than others so the way you rate variety it gradual is simply as a lot as you.

The hassle to bear in thoughts, but, is reading isn't virtually limited to a few thing time you've penciled it into your schedule. As extended as your mind is not tired or distracted, it is continuously up for a hint reading. So take gain of that fact as you're rehearsing your notes to transport the information out of your quick-time period on your lengthy-term memory.

Study Myth #three: Rewrite your notes all all over again.

This one I love. You take notes. You replica the notes you've got were given already taken into your pocket ebook to provide yourself every other suitable look at them. Then you duplicate them onto flash playing cards. If that floats your boat and also you've have been given mounds of loose time that have no longer been allotted in the direction of something else, bypass for it. But if you are like maximum adults who seem to have extra to do than time in which to do it, the concept of spending , 4 or six years rewriting and moving the whole thing you write into another pocket e-book then onto examine gambling playing playing cards seems like lots of wasted time and wooden.

A better concept, I assume, is to take well notes the number one time round. Use your notes to get a better frequently taking place know-how of the underlying concept your professor is laboring to train you and use those notes to piece together the massive picture. Remember, the extra you could relate information to standards, the less difficult the statistics can be to bear in mind.

Study Myth #four: Implement a chain of pre-have a take a look at behavior.

In case you with the aid of hook or through criminal discover five to nine more hours of take a look at time each single day (and thoughts energy collectively with it), there are a few talking heads who assume that in order on your mind – that high-quality, modern, ever-increasing main processing unit – to understand the complex standards you're positive to run into at some point of your university years, you may want to take a seat down down with a pen and a pad and formulate a handful of questions earlier than you ever crack open a ebook. After that, take severa hours reading and rereading fabric then take notes. Got that? Meditate and assume. Read and re-check. Then take notes.

I desire you could see me shaking my head right now. Who has that form of time? Better however, who has that form of interest span? Don't try this. Don't spin your wheels wondering what you may analyze. Reread cloth whilst you want to due to the fact you ignored a few issue. Never as it's a part of a hard method.

This is university. Not NASA. You're now not fixing global starvation. You're fixing math troubles. Do no longer waste treasured time and electricity needlessly toiling (there's that phrase all over again) with tedious practices that upload little or no for your records base and all but get rid of your overall performance. Focus on finding procedures to maximize the time you spend reading, taking notes and reviewing assigned fabric.

Study Myth #five: Plan to spend 2 hours studying in step with week for each credit score hour you take.

That's first-class actual even because it's real. Sometimes you want to make investments more time studying. Sometimes you need less time. One of the hardest courses I ever took have become a one-credit score path. It have emerge as required for my degree software. My professor become a few child genius slightly 5 years older than I turn out to be on the time I took the course. He taught all 4 courses within the series, and every of those 4 semesters, I worked to carry home an A in that beauty. I wasn't the most effective character who struggled in that path. But I come to be one of the most effective university students who had been given an A. I spent about an hour an afternoon on that direction, a far cry from a measly hours every week.

On the turn thing, my intrigue with the history of Rome made a four-credit score rating Greco-Roman course an absolute breeze. I barely keep in mind what the textbook appeared like and I'm but quite the whiz with regards to random facts about the Roman Empire. I didn't spend anywhere close to 8 hours consistent with week reading the fabric. My time investment grow to be an hour or at the most. And I walked away with a few one-of-a-kind nicely-deserved A.

Sit right all the way right down to observe with popularity and intensity then take all the time you need.

five Qualities of an Straight-A Student

So, what does a immediately-A scholar appear to be? A lot together with you, honestly. And like me. Like any oldsters. When it involves instantly-A college college students, it's now not the advent that's consistent. It's those center abilties we noted a touch earlier. Let's take a gander at them.

Integrity is this form of terms that's widely misunderstood. Integrity approach wholeness. It has nothing to do with right and wrong. Integrity is primarily based on a device of putting necessities and following via. It's your capability to make and preserve guarantees to yourself. It's being who you are saying you are and doing what you're announcing you could do.

How integrity performs out academically: You may additionally moreover additionally or won't have a factor-with the aid of way of manner of-component plan for the way you need the next few years to play out, however you do understand you want to graduate near the top of your elegance to offer yourself the most possible options (favored). So you put together your lifestyles and time in a way that ensures you've got got the splendid risk of making exact grades (observe-via).

Self-recognition is a precious tool to should your arsenal. When you are self-conscious, you've got the capability to use custom designed, actual-existence realise-the way to every scenario primarily based on what you realize about your self. Self-cognizance is at its satisfactory while coupled with integrity.

How self-awareness plays out academically: Your preferred television display actually moved to Thursdays. That's going to pose a hassle.

Self-difficulty is quite probable the maximum critical trait right now-A university college students very personal. Self-subject is you exercising manipulate over you. Self-vicinity is the act of shielding yourself accountable. It way subduing your very non-public emotions, whims, desires and weaknesses in pick out of directing your cognizance to undertaking a aim you have set for your self, whether or now not that purpose is large or small.

How energy of will plays out academically: Now that your preferred tv show has moved to Thursdays, you've got a selection to make. To look at or no longer to test? As a terrific deal as it pains you to need to wait to flow into your preferred show, Thursday night time is at the same time as your roommate's out, so it's your most effective take a look at time. Can't danger it. Streaming it is.

Self-motivation is the functionality to interact your personal will to carry out the subjects you have set out to carry out.

Chapter 14: Manage Your Time Without Losing Your Mind

"The key is in not spending time, but in investing it."

~ Stephen R. Covey ~

Focus: Your Most Powerful Asset

Before we jump into the quality techniques to control it gradual, permit's first talk approximately the most powerful asset you have got were given in terms of getting to know check material – attention. We commonly don't assume an excessive amount of approximately popularity and attention. In truth, most folks are on a low eating regimen of the stuff as we purpose to turn out to be more and more proficient within the remarkable artwork of multi-tasking.

News flash. There isn't always this kind of issue as talent in multi-tasking. Your interest is quite limited and lands on one problem at a time. That technique while you're doing subjects proper now, your actual interest and recognition are in a unmarried place while you will be actively taking component in some specific hobby. More frequently than no longer, you're in fact dividing your strength among giving highbrow hobby to at least one factor and directing physical exertion at each distinctive. It's like riding and talking to your cell cellular telephone. When site visitors receives heavy in any other case you want to rapid outmaneuver a big rig and circulate every different lane, you'll because it must be choose out to take a damage from the communique so that it will redirect your highbrow interest from the cellular phone to the street. It's known as toggling. Attention can be toggled. It can not be shared.

It's the equal at the side of your research. That's why it's possible to sit down down for hours inside the the front of an open e-book or plop down on the computer to so-called have a look at then three or 4 hours later, find you've got executed very little. This is known as Cal Newport calls pseudo-analyzing.

Pseudo-studying is what takes region at the same time as you try to engage yourself physical with out enticing your self mentally. The prevent stop result is lots of time spent and strength wasted with out a development to expose for it. The amount of exertions you are able to perform is the direct give up result of the quantity of time you spend strolling and the volume of focus exerted at some point of your allotted artwork time. The masses much less you recognition on what you're studying, the much plenty less you accomplish. The extra you attention on what you're analyzing, the extra you accomplish.

Pseudo-studying is not just a rely of looking to manipulate a wandering mind. Interruptions for your take a look at go with the glide are a massive hassle for lots college students. In less than 3 seconds, an interruption can pull you some distance from your studies and keep your thoughts preoccupied for 15 to 20-5 mins after the interruption passed off. If you've excellent scheduled an hour of study time, 15 minutes of pseudo-reading can decrease your effectiveness through up to 20-five%.

7 Culprits to Watch For

There are seven common culprits that may rapid flip a capacity have a take a look at consultation into pseudo-reading. Be searching for the ones sneaky little hobby killers.

1.Mobile devices. It takes just a few seconds to reply a textual content, but it'll take you a few minutes to recover from the act. Maybe longer if you're searching beforehand to to get a reaction once more.

2.Social media. We take a look at our social feeds constantly. It's an act of dependancy. But again, operating on a pc that alerts you every time a few thing occurs on a social platform is distracting and compromises your overall performance. **As a unique phrase, whether or not or now not your poison is Facebook, Snapchat or a few other social platform, there are instances while you grow to be on social networks and don't have any concept the way you even were given there. It occurs to all and sundry. Well, the very awesome way to break the addiction of senseless social networking is to exchange your passwords to some thing you can now not recollect and keep that statistics someplace on your computer. Remain logged out of the social platform inside the course of the day. That manner you don't come to be spending valuable mins analyzing feeds and looking at photographs till you have got made a aware selection to acquire this.

three.Lack of interest. There are few matters so that you can cause your mind to wander quite like dropping hobby in some factor. Whenever possible, try to discover a few component exciting about what you are analyzing. One of the advantages of reading requirements in lieu of statistics is doing so offers the records context that may be a methods more appealing than honestly rote memorization.

four.Fatigue. Most human beings begin winding down mentally and physical after dinner. Whatever your wind-down time is, that's no longer normally the time to pay attention your efforts on catching up on reading or knocking out the homework. Concentration requires electricity. Study inside the course of the instances if you have the maximum electricity. Study in 40 to 50-minute blocks then take a smash for 10 minutes in advance than you begin your next have a take a look at block.

five.Internal distractions. A busy thoughts is a crowded mind. Do what you can to quiet internal distractions. Internal distractions embody wandering thoughts, starvation, pain or ache. Help yourself to live focused on the project reachable thru maintaining a to-do list nearby. Being reminded of what's for your time finances will assist in keeping you centered.

6.External distractions. Choose a have a look at environment that has minimal visible and auditory distractions. It may additionally seem like a fantastic idea to take a look at out inside the courtyard, but a parade of loads of humans on foot via manner of each hour (with the occasional interruption from parents you recognize in my view) will restriction your potential to stay focused. If your interest wanes as you're gaining information of recent fabric, you received't be able to hold it.

7.Study groups. It's commonplace for a group of four or five college students to get together for extended durations of pseudo-analyzing. They are not in truth socializing, and they'll be not honestly analyzing. You don't need to be on this form of company. If you're searching for to artwork collaboratively with unique university college students, discover a organization of what I name duty partners. An duty companion may be one pupil, a train or a set of college university college students who will maintain you to a excessive preferred of regular overall performance. You can be anticipated to contribute, to have accomplished the analyzing and the homework, and to include fresh mind and suitable questions.

3 Tips For Effective Time Managment

I even have said it in advance than, and I will say it another time. Time is the maximum valuable useful resource any parents has. As lengthy as you have have been given the time to make investments, you can make plans to perform pretty a great deal a few issue. That stated, it's critical that lets in you to recognize the way to control some time. This segment of the e-book is designed to equip you with a fixed of capabilities as a manner to in the long run keep you responsible as to how you're using it sluggish and could serve that will help you stay on on-assignment so you can do what needs to be performed precisely how it wishes to be finished while it wishes to be completed.

Write matters down

It's a high-quality idea to increase the dependancy of writing topics down, and I'll inform you why. Creating a seen inventory of the duties to your to-do listing frees your thoughts from the challenge of getting to keep in mind all of it. In case you haven't discovered, to-do lists in no way appear to go away. From daily, the gadgets at the listing might also additionally furthermore change, however it's a perpetual cycle of together with and eliminating devices. Let your operating memory off the hook through solving those obligations onto a tangible medium that you can speak to inside the route of the day with out an excessive amount of intellectual try.

Next, list-making is a topic that allows you to set up your private, expert and academic duties into the 24-hour region of in some unspecified time in the future. This permits you to get a practical visible of what your day looks like. Once you have got were given the whole lot written down, you may quite plenty are expecting what you may and will no longer be able to get finished, and you could offer you with short and dirty techniques for buying greater matters accomplished in any given 24-hour duration. You are far less probably to overbook it sluggish by way of the use of crowding your agenda with responsibilities which may be basically meaningless. You are much more likely to fill in gaps with critical duties if you discover you have got were given were given beneath-booked it gradual.

When you write topics down, you may with out issue add new responsibilities on your listing and circulate incomplete duties to a more reachable time later inside the week, so matters don't slip thru the cracks. At the give up of the day, your list of finished duties covered with checks is a reward that maximum folks will see as ok motivation to hold making lists and getting increasingly topics finished.

Create Rituals

Habits and rituals circulate hand in hand. We will be predisposed to apply every day rituals to our behavior to motive them to extra a laugh. For instance, your morning run is genuinely as effective at keeping you in shape in case you run in silence. But if you've put together a butt-kicking soundtrack for your morning run, the act of consisting of tune in your dependancy of strolling turns into part of the ritual you lease to up the leisure element of your exercising regular.

You are going to have a observe. You already recognise the addiction of studying is critical for your instructional achievement. The environment you create, lighting fixtures you use, song you play, snacks you've got got got accessible and a few different ceremonious sports activities you may upload to your reading turns into a part of your have a look at ritual.

Rituals can encompass any form of activities you operate every single time you look at. Their cause is to inspire you and limit the motives you have not to look at. Rituals assist to address any vulnerabilities which can display up as part of your regular take a look at conduct.

Let's say Wednesday is your most hard day. Starting first factor in the morning, you've have been given returned-to-over again instructions until mid-afternoon, determined by means of the usage of a one-hour tutoring consultation. You also can pick to have a short, one-hour have a take a look at session at the same time as you get home within the early night. But you realize that in case you eat your normal dinner earlier than you test, you're going to be tired.

So your Wednesday night time have a look at ritual can also include grabbing an coffee and a foot-prolonged sub at the manner domestic so that you can snack as you look at. This ritual will assist reduce the temptation of getting a massive, comforting meal after a long day then passing out in the scholar lounge with a e book to your face. And due to the fact you're worn-out and your interest also can already be compromised, Wednesday night time is your night time time to examine at your table wearing earbuds that block out any sounds which may additionally distract you and cause you to get off undertaking.

Rituals may be something. Just make sure to craft your rituals, in order that they propel your educational success. Avoid any sports activities that might upload on your frustrations or sluggish your productivity.

Delay procrastination

You recognise this already, however I'm going to tell you besides. Procrastinating is counter-inexperienced. In a exquisite global, there would be a perpetual feel of ease in doing some issue desires to be achieved. But we don't stay in a fantastic global, so we need to have interaction our strength of will to finish a few sports activities.

Willpower is a notable trouble. We all have it, and it in no manner runs low. But we do have a say on whether or now not we use it. Often the selection not to workout energy of will to complete a undertaking effects in procrastination.

Procrastination is hard. We procrastinate due to the fact we delude ourselves into thinking our destiny selves will someway be capable of exercise the challenge our gift selves are unwilling to exercise. In fact, field is a muscle that have to be regularly exercised in order for it to be powerful. The electricity of the following day's region depends cautiously on your willingness to be disciplined today. So if you're wondering, "Today, I'm heading to the films. Tomorrow, I'll conquer the sector!" you're going to be upset while the morrow comes.

So, how do you avoid procrastinating? Courage. Believe it or not, procrastination is an avoidance method. We use procrastination to deal with subjects that make us uncomfortable. By heading off the project, we're rewarded with a short revel in of comfort. We procrastinate with the cause of minimizing our tension, but procrastination comes with a serving of anxiety of a great type – the abiding focus that there are belongings you want to do which you haven't finished but.

Don't permit procrastination burden you. Adopt a proactive mindset that says if there may be some thing to be carried out, you're going to do it. That approach in case your to-do list includes 15 unimportant obligations and one large important element, do the only big essential problem first even if it takes a extra time funding than the 15 unimportant responsibilities combined.

If you have already advanced the dependancy of procrastinating, it's going to be a tough dependancy to break. You have to reprogram your mind to apprehend the quick-lived experience of consolation you get from maintaining off an hobby is menial in contrast to the burden you supply via being continuously aware about the truth that you have unfinished enterprise employer that dreams your interest.

Take this domestic approximately procrastinating: The experience of fulfillment you get from starting and completing a project is a miles higher praise than the brief comfort you get via the usage of averting it.

Chapter 15: How to Create a Time Budget

Your time finances is your every day log of methods you use it sluggish to fulfill your duties. Creating it requires a one-hour time funding on the first Friday of each new semester and about 5 minutes a day to keep.

New semester budgeting

At the start of every semester, make a grasp calendar that is seen from your desk. I would possibly suggest shopping for a huge wall calendar that may effortlessly be seen from pretty masses anywhere in the room. The duration is important because it will function a visible reminder of any upcoming educational, non-public or professional responsibilities which is probably no longer going to exchange.

Your first line of safety to shield it gradual and stave off mediocrity starts offevolved offevolved on the first Friday of the brand new semester. Sit down collectively with your syllabus and a massive wall calendar to grow to be aware about and word any vital dates.

These encompass assignments, papers, test dates, the dates of any extra-curricular sports that require a while, massive college activities (any you need to wait, at least), college breaks and another dates you want to take into account.

For every main paper, quiz or examination indexed inside the syllabus, word in your calendar each the sort of educational responsibility and the share of your grade for which it money owed. This is an important seen reason. Seeing the phrases "Exam 35%" stuffed in a square will likely feature suitable enough motivation to hold you from squandering a while due to the fact the take a look at date attracts near.

Weekly research plan

Once you've got added all the crucial dates in your calendar, take note of any research papers which can be due. Now is the time to create a studies plan. On a separate sheet of paper, create a heading for every week of the semester then fill in a research plan for the complete semester based on any research tasks you'll be required to expose in over the path of the semester. Decide proper now what number of hours you can make investments in line with week - beginning that second week of college - in getting the studies and writing executed for those papers.

So the primary 4 weeks of university, your research plan will appearance something like this:

Week 1 - Sept 3

∞Humanities / Mozart –teens and education (2hr)

Week 2 – Sept 10

∞Humanities / Mozart - Prodigious works to youngster years (2hr)

Week 3 – Sept 17

∞Humanities / Mozart – Social and political climate inside the route of early life (90m)

∞Psych / Anger Management – Forming identity, Mike Fisher (90m)

Week 4 – Sept 24

∞Humanities / Mozart – Early maturity (90m)

∞Psych / Anger Management –Core beliefs (90m)

This step is important for two motives. First, it permits you to paintings continuously in the course of task your purpose without the strain of scrambling round on the final minute and attempting to tug A-diploma exercise consultation of skinny air. Second, it offers you sufficient time to alter your time desk in case you find the undertaking don't forget amount requires extra effort than you in the beginning planned.

Your subsequent line of defense in opposition to mediocrity is to cement studies and writing time for big papers into your schedule at the day of your lightest workload. You want to feature this on your calendar as a tough and fast appointment because an venture that is due weeks from now's a pinnacle purpose for procrastination. Don't even tempt your self that way. Make studies a standing appointment to which you faithfully file every unmarried week until all papers are completed, and you've got were given your A-paper to your hand.

Daily time Budgeting

Since your center instructional, private and expert duties are not going to exchange at a few degree in the rest of the semester, your very last line of safety in opposition to mediocrity is each day protection. This genuinely includes growing a list of helping desires and scheduling them into your day earlier than you go away inside the mornings.

Your dreams are to gain a four.Zero-grade aspect not unusual and hold a properly-balanced social existence. Your helping objectives can be contemplated inside the responsibilities on your to-do list, as most of your duties will go toward making sure the ones dreams are met. That manner your to-do list will encompass by and large homework, have a examine time, reading, take a look at sessions, doing the laundry, social sports activities activities, attending video games, and another interest that desires to healthy into your lifestyles on a every day foundation.

Got all that? Now proper here's the clean detail. Every day, take 5 minutes to iron out what desires to be eliminated from and taken to your to-do listing. Success philosophers encourage planners to generally plan the day's sports activities the night time time earlier than. The wondering behind that is creating a list at night time time time lets in your thoughts to visit work locating out the information of the manner to get the topics in your list carried out. It thoroughly can be that while you wake up in the morning, you'll have concept of smarter methods to perform the matters for your list. Of path, in case you choose to do your list within the morning, revel in unfastened. The give up stop end result should quite an awful lot be the identical.

Your time fee range is a chronological list of the day's obligations. Include each the call of the task and the time allocated for that project. This master list need to additionally encompass any commands or extra-curricular sports you can attend that day. It is a seen illustration of your calendar so you can see exactly wherein some time goes and you could realise precisely how a whole lot time you need to get things completed. It additionally gives you the threat to weave a seamless flow into your day that continues you moving earlier.

For instance, when you have library books to head returned and some time table's no longer taking you anywhere close to the library nowadays, you can maintain in thoughts there's a return field at the sidewalk proper outdoor the Chemistry constructing. It makes experience, then to pencil in "Library books" to get up proper earlier than "Chem magnificence." You slightly have to interrupt a stride as drop off your books and walk into the constructing.

Your time price range ought to be clean to keep. It doesn't take an elegantly crafted, hand-stitched planner. Just a pen and a 1/2 sheet of paper. It's the excellent manner to control your complex life. When subjects arise and a few aspect at the listing goes undone, in reality add it to the agenda for each exclusive day this week. When the professor drops a contemporary task on you that's due Friday, scribble a short observe each beside your listing or on the again of your list so that you can upload that homework time in your agenda sooner or later this week.

Craft some time price range, so it offers you with a reminder of what desires to be completed similarly to the most inexperienced technique for buying subjects finished. And if at any time you wander far from some time budget and the complete gadget goes to hell, whilst you're organized to re-up, go to hell and retrieve it. You can select out up in that you left off without missing a beat. Be Flexible Be Realistic

In order on your time rate range to work, you genuinely do should toe the line among maintaining flexibility and keeping the field crucial to preserve up your momentum, so that you don't slip again into vintage conduct. If there are blocks of time to your ordinary time table in which you are bodily or mentally exhausted, this is absolutely not the time to stress your self to have a look at. An athlete, as an instance, may additionally find out that during the 60 minutes right away following workout she desires a recuperation length. There's no disgrace in that. Even if the recuperation duration is actually sitting on the sofa looking tv, if that's the excellent use of her time and electricity at that 2nd, her time rate range want to consist of an hour-lengthy recovery duration.

Remember, you're budgeting each some time and your strength. If you have got one however no longer the opportunity, you'll still be considerably ineffective if you attempt to use that space of time for some thing other than a healing length.

You want to furthermore plan for the sudden. Okay, so that you can't simply plan for the unexpected, but you can modify some time price range to house sudden activities and rethink how and whilst to perform the subjects that went undone as a prevent quit end result.

Your time finances have to consist of any time constraints you can currently have. Address time constraints with the eager understanding that everybody has them. Account for blocks of time in that you're really unavailable and upload them on your time finances on the instances even as they're relevant. The goal is to usually have a sensible image of your possible hours and discover smart strategies to art work in a few unspecified time inside the future of these instances.

Beware of 1 downside collectively collectively together with your time price range – overbooking a while. It's ok to squeeze some extra topics into the price range once in a while. But making it a addiction can effortlessly motive burnout. It will allow you to hold a bit of perspective if at the least as quickly as a month, you are taking stock of your academic, professional and personal responsibilities to ensure they'll be aligned at the side of your desires. Anything that doesn't align together with your goals reduce it off. Doing so will assist you to live on top of things of some time, so you in no way get to the aspect where you sense like your life is a runaway educate.

Use downtime for your benefit

There's no time like downtime to examine. When you think of downtime, you can conjure up pix of camping out within the front of the television, hoping for a wonderful film. But you moreover mght have downtime scattered in some unspecified time within the future of your day in tiny chunks. You have 45 seconds of downtime even as you're brushing your teeth, 5 mins of downtime within the bathe. Maybe 25 or half of-hour of downtime at the same time as you're exercising. This is precious observe time if you use it.

You're now not going to tote alongside your textbook for your morning run, however it's no longer a horrible concept to change out your workout soundtrack for a recording of the previous day's Psych lecture. You can also even want to be aware of recorded lectures within the mornings as you have got end up geared up for sophistication. It doesn't genuinely recall what you do. The factor is to take the ones sporadic chunks of mins and seconds and squeeze in a bit learning.

Here's a tip even though to help make your take a look at time a piece greater tolerable. Skip recording audio of stupid professors. You survived their prolonged, dry lectures as quickly as. Don't placed your self thru that again. If audio is a superb test technique for you, seize some sound bites from the professors who are a piece extra engaging. Otherwise, you can thoroughly music the audio out. For your dull professors, you can discover your textbook and your very own handwritten notes are a much higher trainer. Hey, it takes location.

Want to capitalize on that downtime? Here's wherein to locate it:

∞During your morning rest room recurring

∞At the breakfast desk

∞On your manner to beauty /campus

∞While you're in your chair looking forward to beauty to begin

∞Between commands

∞Waiting in line for lunch

∞Eating lunch

∞While you're exercising

∞While you're doing chores or tidying up your residing region

∞While you're at artwork

∞In the 5 mins earlier than you take a seat all the manner right right down to eat dinner

∞During your overdue night time time time relaxation room routine

Even if each of the above-listed sports best took you 5 mins to carry out, you will however carve out a similarly 60 mins of unscheduled have a have a look at time over the path of the day that takes little or no effort to in fact do.

Just a few minutes right here and there of reviewing notes or paying attention to audio. If you have been to do that on a every day basis together with your maximum tough beauty, you will upload each different 5 hours of have a observe time to your arsenal. That can be definitely sufficient more time to keep you inside the ninety two% – a hundred% range.

Chapter 16: No weekends required

Now, assuming you're heeding those precious time management tips and clearly giving interest to managing a while, your Monday through Friday grind (or Sunday thru Thursday grind) goes to be enough time to get the entirety achieved that wants to be finished. Your common 5-day workweek offers you with a hundred and twenty hours to use as you notice wholesome and breaks down approximately like this:

∞35 hours for sleep

∞30 hours of observe time

∞30 hours of personal time

∞15 hours of sophistication time

∞5 hours for adventure

∞five hours for meals

I based completely the take a look at time hours on the antique adage that you want to count on to do hours of tough work for each credit score rating hour for that you are enrolled. In my mind, six hours of have a look at time in step with day is a steep time funding, however it takes location, mainly with university students who make a addiction of pseudo-analyzing.

Still, the element of this listing is to demonstrate that beyond sleep time and class time; you have got were given an additional 70 hours consistent with week to apply in your time price range. Of direction, such things as sports sports sports and in addition-curricular sports activities activities will possibly be pulled out of your private time, however do the arithmetic. That's 14 hours in line with day to satisfy your non-public, expert and academic duties and you never need to touch your weekend hours.

PART THREE

Tactics That Work

"In a 2008 survey of extra than a hundred and sixty,000 undergraduates enrolled inside the University of California device, university

165

college students were asked to listing what interferes most with their academic achievement… The number one reason, agreed upon through 33 percent of college college students, who stated they struggled with one specific trouble 'frequently' or 'all the time': They certainly did not recognize a way to take a seat down down and have a have a have a look at."

~ Keith O'Brien ~

~ The Boston Globe ~

It's easy sufficient to understand you want to study extra. But the data are in, about a 3rd of the college college students surveyed don't even apprehend a way to do that effectively. So we're going to begin this segment with actionable techniques to get you hitting the books and seeing results. Before we get to the red meat, permit's set the desk.

In the very last phase, I talked a piece approximately the significance of staying prepared on the identical time as you examine. Before you are taking a seat all of the way down to check, you truly need to understand wherein everything is. Just much like the neighborhood handyman isn't going to spend 5 or ten mins looking for a screwdriver (or worse, display as masses because the undertaking without one), you need to understand in which to discover your gadget of the exchange. They must be and now not using a trouble to be had.

But beyond having an area to place your pencils, you furthermore may also want to make sure you placed into impact a smooth filing gadget to stock any assignments that have been graded and over again to you.

Graded assignments are a useful examine device for financial disaster checks, your midterm and the very last. Not most effective that, you may use any comments written for your assignments to benefit perception into how your professor thinks and the extent of ordinary standard overall performance she or he expects from you.

If you ever collect an mission once more with feedback you don't understand, get clarity proper now. If you don't apprehend your professor's notes, you chance making the equal mistake once more on every other mission and possibly being graded more harshly for it. Ideally, at the equal time because the give up of the semester rolls spherical, you need that lets in you to are waiting for your final grade indoors some percentage factors. Keep tune of your private grades, so there aren't any ugly surprises at the give up of the time period.

It ought to skip without saying

There are primary success thoughts you want to recognize for college. Perhaps they have to circulate with out saying, however I am going to say them besides.

Go to all scheduled training and labs. No kidding. It may additionally moreover appear like you have all the opportunities within the international to get to the following beauty, however for each class you skip over, there's a terrific threat you omitted a few precious records so that it will show up in question form on a check in some unspecified time within the future inside the course of the semester.

"I can get the equal statistics from the ebook," you can say. Yes. But you gained't recognize what your professor thinks are the maximum important components of the fabric provided within the e-book without showing up for class. That sort of perception is often observed at a few degree within the lecture.

The different college primary achievement precept is to attend to yourself. Sorry, but waxy noodles floating in salt water are not mind food. They barely pass as meals. I suppose they formally fall into the meals class, as a remember of fact. Do what you may to capture some vitamins among junk meals outings, or as a minimum, add a multi-eating regimen to your each day nutrients plan.

And I apprehend you're wild and unfastened, pretty likely for the very first time, however you continue to want sleep. Well, your mind goals sleep, at the least. Your body can bypass for days without sleep, but one night of omitted sleep and your cognitive mind feature will slow down substantially.

In order to feature optimally, your brain wishes vitamins and time to recharge. That time comes within the form of sleep. The amount of sleep you need varies from man or woman to individual. Some humans characteristic flawlessly nicely on 4 to five hours of sleep. Other human beings also can want seven or eight hours of sleep. Whatever your magic amount can be, get the quantity of sleep you need to perform your nice. No extra, no less.

Your mind is a small organ, but it uses a huge quantity of the power you eat – about 20%. In order for your cognitive mind to perform obligations like questioning, speaking and remembering, it truly has to get enough sleep. College achievement turns into especially now not feasible at the same time as your capability to assume, cause and take into account are compromised. And now…

Your Crash Course in How to Study

I began this e-book with the aid of pronouncing something startling, and this is through the usage of, and big, far too many college university students appear to gain on campus ill-prepared to satisfy the wishes of college-degree reading. The first part of this ebook helped you to get a cope with on your strengths and weaknesses. The second element supplied you with a element-through-point technique for managing it sluggish. In issue 3 of this e-book, it's all about developing the tactical skills to truly do college-diploma art work. We will begin with analyzing.

What is studying?

Studying is the method of directing awareness, time and power to studying, knowledge and remembering statistics. It is the steady and enthusiastic pursuit of facts, a method to an forestall. Studying is usually preceded with the resource of the usage of goal-placing and desires can variety from the usage of Wikipedia to determine out what happened in previous seasons of a popular television show you're simply starting to observe to spending four years hitting the books to build up the understanding had to earn an undergraduate diploma.

The intensity (quantity of focus exerted in terms of the time spent) of your reading is at once related to the dreams you are trying to reap. In the above example of catching up on a tv display, the Wikipedia article will be the quantity of your study strive. But for you, the vastness of the fabric you should grasp so you can gain your purpose of earning that degree manner you need to technique analyzing with a specific plan and follow a tough and speedy of milestones alongside the manner.

Creating a check plan

Consistency is the important factor to victory with reference to growing a look at plan. Consistency way for every of your lessons; you've got a fixed have a look at time desk in which you are capable of positioned your self on a constant weight-reduction plan of statistics and mind. Lots of university university college students make their claim to repute cramming the night time time earlier than a take a look at and faring pretty properly. But we already mentioned what takes location to the data you are taking in at the same time as you great need it for a few hours. Your mind will sell off it, not file it. Unfortunately, which means that the subsequent time you need to get admission to that information (say, for the midterm), there's an incredible chance it acquired't be there. You'll need to cram again.

Your university training is constructed incrementally, precept upon principle. So there are only a few schooling you may take in which exercise the selection to sell off the records you obtain is your first-rate preference. Your time and strength are constrained, and due to the fact they're each valuable assets, you want to use them wisely. Create a look at plan and address any have a examine time you time desk as a state of affairs.

Your test plan and some time finances match collectively like puzzle portions. In truth, while you take a seat down down at the begin of the semester to create your wall calendar and outline a studies technique, you have already began developing a have a examine plan. The only problem left to do is allocate observe time for every elegance. At the begin of the semester, this could take a few practice. It's like I said in advance than – some material might be much less complex to apprehend than other cloth. So you may find you need to tweak your take a look at plan some times if you need to make it satisfactory.

Make reading a concern

Now, be warned. Study plans only work in case you art work them. That way the have a take a look at time you schedule has to become non-negotiable. Once you sit down down down at your table, spark off your computer or positioned pen to pad, live centered on the project handy until it's miles accomplished. Don't solution any calls. Don't get distracted. Don't paintings with the tv on or have any tune with lyrics gambling in the ancient beyond. Only take breaks at the give up of the hour then straight away get decrease again to art work at the same time as your 10- or 15-minute damage is over.

Another issue to take into account is immersion works exceptional at the same time as it's completed over an prolonged time period. So strive not to time desk an entire day in which you handiest take a look at one problem. You will actually be in a better function to undergo in thoughts what you examine whilst you take a look at more than one subjects over the route of the day.

Secrets from the Front of the Class

What do straight away-A college college students comprehend which you don't? A few matters. So allow's speak about a handful of easy strategies and secrets and techniques and techniques from the the the front of the beauty.

Make friends

One potential many right now-A college students cultivate that others may moreover go away to threat is deliberately retaining relationships with specific A college college students. Part of the fun of college is building social relationships. Savvy students leverage those relationships for educational advantage as well.

Chapter 17: Taking Smart Lecture Notes

Good lecture notes will lessen your private study time down notably and help you 0 in on precisely what you need to apprehend an exquisite manner to do nicely in your elegance. Here are the three keys to correct observe-taking.

1. Active listening

Most human beings aren't awesome listeners and agree with it or now not, listening is quite difficult to do. It takes area. For a number of us, what we name listening is definitely a number of diverse subjects. Sometimes while we appearance to others like we're listening, we're simply geared up to talk. Other instances our minds are preoccupied, so our interest is divided. Sometimes we're just now not interested by what the speaker is saying so we listen to the rhythm of his or her speech and the cadence of his or her voice, so we recognize on the equal time as to reply, however in reality, we weren't without a doubt listening.

Listening calls for the kind of awareness and interest which you supply to studying. It's tuning out the conversations round you and refusing to be distracted via a person else strolling thru. It's having the capacity to inform the alternative person precisely what she or he said each verbatim or on your non-public terms and being capable of offer an engaged and knowledgeable reaction to what has been said. It's setting the degree for a talk in vicinity of leaving the other person on degree to deliver a monologue.

Active listening in elegance is even more tough, in element because of the truth it is a monologue and now not a talk. The professor isn't doing a good deal of some thing to make the presentation greater thrilling, and simply often the professor is rattling off statistics like he's finished a thousand times earlier than. Still, to be able to take actual notes, you need to get fairly accurate at energetic listening. That technique information what to write down and what to bypass over. That technique knowledge how your professor gives data and how he offers the information that he thinks is most treasured, compared to how he provides one-of-a-type records. It manner paying attention to the nuances of the professor's presentation, but, silly it is able to appear.

2. Focus on getting to know, no longer writing

Taking notes is prepared amassing the maximum essential records and writing it down. It isn't about finding some brilliant way to write down down down everything phrase that escapes the professor's mouth. So you need to be careful now not to slide into stenographer mode. If you keep up with the studying, you may have all the information you'll ever want on any given trouble. What your professor affords is context and perspective. That's what you want to install writing down down.

Don't waste some time scribbling a gaggle of facts that you may turn out to be having to have a examine later. Remember, the more you understand the underlying due to this and relevance of the material the less tough it'll likely be to synthesize the information later. I truely have stated a few instances that in case you attend the in-elegance lectures, you can reduce down drastically for your non-public have a examine time. That's authentic great in case you attention on getting to know eventually of class time.

** Every now after which, you get a professor who appears to be regurgitating the ebook verbatim. When this is the case – and you're going to like this – bypass the reading. You're getting a better price from the professor in the shape of context, records, and perception into what is going to be emphasized on the test. Save your self the hassle of sitting down some hours per week to have foreknowledge of a few issue the professor is going to end up announcing anyway. If you are trying to determine among doing the reading at home and possibly skipping the magnificence altogether, go to the class. Skip the at-domestic reading. **

3. Organize your notes

When you are certainly centered on writing down the principles, conclusions, and questions, you possibly gained't need to take greater time to rewrite your notes. If you're scribbling records at lightning pace everywhere within the internet net page, you'll simply want to perform a touch organizing afterward. If you're seeking out context, it's going to likely be much less complex to live prepared.

Consider the usage of as a minimum particular shades of ink or the usage of a pen and a highlighter as you are taking notes. You have that allows you to study your notes and distinguish the questions from the answers, both through the use of the manner the data is formatted at the net internet web page (indenting answers, for instance) or by using using using the color code you've used to distinguish one magnificence of data from some extraordinary.

Get to Know Your Professor

One trouble all immoderate-performers have in commonplace is the willingness to invite questions and maintain the strains of verbal exchange open the various scholar and the teacher. In excessive school, there might also additionally were a person who did that type of issue for you. In university, you're on your very personal. That's a terrific detail. The functionality to talk, set up rapport and art work collaboratively to treatment issues is an crucial center competency to demonstrate in the job marketplace. Stop hiding

One of the maximum risky conduct you may undertake to negatively impact your college education is maintaining off challenges. Challenges gift themselves in some of techniques, like knowing you need assist and no longer getting it. Often human beings –

not just university college students – who're extra concerned with their image than their productivity sabotage both at the same time as they are reluctant to are looking for assist once they want it. Let me will let you know right now; that thoughts-set isn't going to fly.

There might be instances even as you want extra help and a chunk more steerage. There can be subjects which is probably greater tough with a view to draw close than others. You want to have the intestinal fortitude to raise your hand or ask a query in the route of class time if you have the opportunity to invite. Chances are, in case you aren't willing to invite your query at a few degree within the ordinary elegance time, you obtained't find time for your schedule to discover your professor at some stage in administrative center hours each.